The Althouse Press

Bailey / *The Girls Are the Ones*
With the Pointy Nails

The Girls Are the Ones With the Pointy Nails

An Exploration of Children's Conceptions of Gender

Karen R. Bailey

THE ALTHOUSE PRESS

First published in 1993 by
THE ALTHOUSE PRESS
Acting Dean: B.B. Kymlicka
Director of The Press: J. Sanders
Faculty of Education, The University of Western Ontario,
1137 Western Road, London, Ontario, Canada N6G 1G7

Edited by Don Gutteridge

Editorial Assistant: Katherine Mayhew
Cover: Louise Gadbois, U.W.O. Graphic Services

Canadian Cataloguing in Publication Data

Bailey, Karen R., 1954-
  The girls are the ones with the pointy nails

Includes bibliographical references and index.
ISBN 0-920354-35-1

1. Sex differences - Study and teaching (Primary).
2. Sex differences in literature - Study and
teaching (Primary). 3. Sex role in children.
4. Cognition in children. I. Title.

HQ57.3.B35 1993   372.3'72   C93-094743-6

Printed and bound in Canada by Kromar Printing Ltd., 725 Portage Avenue,
Winnipeg, Manitoba R3G 0M8.

To my first teacher: my mother,
who showed me the joys of reading, writing, and thinking.

CONTENTS

Acknowledgements

It should be noted that, although parental permission to participate in the study was obtained for all students, to ensure their anonymity I have changed the names of the children. Although I am unable to recognize each family personally, I remain indebted to both the parents who so willingly shared their children, and the children who showed me the value of listening to what they have to say.

I have been fortunate to benefit from the wisdom of two advisors, Sharon Rich and Barbara Houston, who offered constructive suggestions on numerous drafts, and provided ongoing support and friendship throughout the writing process. I am also indebted to Don Gutteridge whose editing voice not only carefully matched my own, but often improved upon it. Thanks goes to Katherine Mayhew for both her meticulous proofing and the time she spent on the overall shape of the book. The encouragement provided by Aniko Varpalotai, along with several other faculty members from both the University of Western Ontario and the Ontario Institute for Studies in Education has also been appreciated.

Both the research process and my classroom practice were strengthened by the knowledge of Pina Pucci, whose understanding of children complemented my own, as we shared the "ups and downs" of ten classes of preschoolers. June Doan and Bill Yates graciously allowed me access to their thoughts, their teaching practices, and the children in their classrooms. Doug Acton, Brenda McKelvey-Donner, and Mary Vernon provided the administrative support essential to a project such as this one. With a minimum of stress over lost data, Pat Snyders ensured that the computer accurately reflected my thoughts and ideas. To these and other friends and colleagues who have significantly affected my thinking by listening, challenging, and discussing, a special thank you.

And finally, I must acknowledge the many children who have spontaneously shared their thoughts and dreams with me. By demanding acceptance of their knowledge, they represent much more than the data from which my thinking has evolved. They are truly the ones who own the vision of a better future.

Preface

It is a common belief that teachers strive for 'the teachable moment', that happy moment when the children sit attentively, their minds tuned to the wisdom the teacher is about to impart. Early in my own career, I realized that in the teaching of four-year-olds, such moments are few and far between; for the children are much too busy creating 'learnable moments', as they explore their own interpretations of the world around them. This is not to imply that young children do not pay attention to adult opinions, but rather that there is no guarantee they will accord them more value than their own thoughts and feelings. As a result, I've learned to pay careful attention to children's conversations, as I attempt to discover how they arrive at their own conclusions.

One such teacher-learning session is guaranteed each time I introduce a curriculum unit on "Birth and Babies" to a class of four-year-olds. The discussion, although initiated by the teacher, seldom remains in my hands as the children eagerly shout out answers, and begin arguing amongst themselves.

> **So who can tell me the difference between girl babies and boy babies?**
> - That's easy. You don't have to tell 'cause the doctor will tell you.
> - Yeah. He knows. He holds the baby upside down and says, "It's a girl!"
> - No, no. He does it like this (*demonstrates*). And then he says, "Mommy and daddy, you have a boy!"
> **But how does the doctor know?**
> - He just does. That's his job. To look at the baby and say what

it is. So moms and dads just have to remember what the doctor says.

- Well, I think the doctor knows 'cause he looks at the baby's clothes. If they're pink, then it's a girl. If they're blue, it's a boy.
- No way! When a baby's born, it doesn't have any clothes on. (*giggles*) It's born naked!
- Well then, the mom just looks at the hair. Girls have long hair and boys have short.
- Some boy babies are bald. My cousin is bald and he's a boy. His dad is bald, too.

Can girl babies be born bald?

- Nah. Girl babies are born with bonnets on. Pink, frilly ones.
- Some girls have bows in their hair when they're born.
- Girls cry, too. Boy babies are strong so they don't cry as much.
- Well, I still think it's easier to ask the doctor. Or the mom. Moms know everything!

Participation in open-ended class discussions such as this one, along with time spent observing young children in a variety of settings, has increased my knowledge about young children's understanding of gender. Paying attention to such 'learnable moments' has taught me that young children are emphatic in their beliefs and eager to share what they know with anyone who provides the opportunity. I've learned that children's beliefs are rooted in their day-to-day experiences, and that they base their assumptions on the perceived behaviour of the models within their environment. Furthermore, I've become convinced that, on many occasions, children view themselves as being right, and do not necessarily acknowledge limitations to the knowledge that they have. By actively participating in these discussions, I've also learned that children's perceptions can be modified, not because 'the teacher says it's so', but because their understanding increases with the introduction of new material from a variety of sources.

The study described in this book is the end result of many hours spent in discussions with young children about gender-related issues. Although my thinking originated out of my own need to understand the behavioural differences I noted between boys and girls, it was fueled by my concerns about the effects of these differences on the classroom community I was creating. And while my interest eventually led to a formal study which explores in depth children's conceptions of gender, my interpretation of the data collected and my suggestions for change have been strongly influenced by time spent observing and listening to the children in my classes.

The study, itself, explores children's conceptions of gender in response to literature that presents non-conventional gender behaviours. Specifically, the language examined by the study includes children's oral discussion of four literature selections in response to teacher-guided questions about the gendered behaviours of the story characters.

A review of recent research indicates the educational need for a study such as this. Because of a lack of relevant research on the effects of stereotyping within educational programs for young children, there is a need to develop studies that focus on young children's conceptions of gender. Because gender is based in the language children learn, it is important to examine children's understanding of gender through the oral language they produce. In this study, children's oral language production thus becomes a major focus. It is only by first gaining an understanding of the way that children perceive gender that we can hope to design learning situations which will encourage children to question stereotypic beliefs.

During the course of the study, I undertook to:

- describe children's conceptions of gender as expressed in their responses to literature chosen specifically because it presents behaviours that are at odds with conventional gender roles;
- examine the differences in the ways that girls and boys perceive gender;
- draw conclusions about the implications of evaluating children's conceptions of gender for educational programs for young children.

The book is organized as follows. The first chapter outlines more fully how I came to do the study, including my perceived role as teacher-researcher, my evolving interest in gender issues, and the reasoning behind the educational need for a study such as this one. Chapter 2 describes the methodology used in the study, including the rationale for analyzing children's responses to literature within a classroom setting. Chapters 3 and 4 analyze the data transcribed from the children's responses to the literature selections, in the context of related research. Chapters 5 through 7 address the implications of the findings for the field of education, with specific reference to educational programs for young children.

Based on my own experiences, I realize that making the jump from other people's research to one's own classroom practice is never an easy one. Because readers will come to this book with varying experiences and expectations, they will necessarily leave it with differing conclusions. Many will have already noted the important role gender plays within classroom practice and will be seeking ideas for program implementation. Others will be fascinated by children's gendered behaviours and will be wondering whether their observations are important enough to act upon. Still others may not yet feel the need to challenge children's existing beliefs about gender. Whichever perspective applies, I hope each reader is intrigued enough to explore those 'learnable moments' that children so readily offer, and in doing so, to take the time to test out an idea or two.

1 / Breaking New Ground

It's easy to tell which are the girls and which are the boys; the girls are the ones with the pointy nails. *Jill / 4*

At first glance, an unobtrusive visitor to a classroom where young children are busily engaged in their chosen form of play-work may not notice overt differences in the behaviours of the boys and the girls. The children seem to be randomly scattered around the room, with no apparent sex differentiation in their chosen groupings. Both girls and boys enact domestic scenes in the house-centre and create masterpieces at the paint-easels. Children of both sexes are involved in the building of block structures, while others fly airplanes around the room.

Chances are, however, if that same visitor takes the time to listen to the children's conversations and to question them about their activities, differences associated with the children's understanding of the play of boys and girls will become apparent. Of the boys in the house-centre, one is a burglar stealing the baby, while the other is a police officer making an arrest; the girls playing beside them are wives and mothers (and thus made powerless through the boys' fantasy?). As the boys build a block airport, the girls create a restaurant within it, complete with play food for the male pilots and female flight attendants. While the girls paint pictures of suns and rainbows, the boys' art work shows 'superhero' figures killing 'bad guys'.

The point raised by this scenario is that in order to create educational programs which are sensitive to the influences of gender, we must first pay attention to children's conceptions of appropriate gender behaviours. Although on the surface the play behaviours of girls and boys may appear similar, underneath, children are acting out distinct roles which they traditionally associate with one specific sex.

The purpose of this study, then, is to explore young children's conceptions of gender by listening to the stories that they tell, and by questioning them about the ways they think boys and girls should act. Literature selections, shared within the classroom context, provide the stimulus for encouraging children to talk about gender; however, it is the children themselves who tell the 'real' stories, providing through their conversations insights into the ways they think about gender-related issues. The intensity of young children's developing beliefs about boys and girls, their sensitivity about gender issues, and the means by which they resolve the gender-related conflicts within their world may provide us with a better understanding of how they perceive their own genderedness. Before turning to a formal description of the study, however, there is another important story to be told.

Coming to the Research

Learning About Children

Like many beginning teachers, I came to teaching with the expectation that children were miniature versions of adults, anxiously awaiting their turn to receive pre-selected knowledge. Thus, on the first day of September, I arrived at my classroom door with a picture in my mind of children as rows of empty vessels waiting to be filled with the knowledge gleaned from the curriculum 'bibles' stacked on my desk. When lesson after lesson was interrupted by childish chatter, I realized that the vessels in my classroom were not only already full, but were brimming over with child-chosen knowledge. "Teacher, guess where I went last night? To the fair and my brother threw up on the spinning ride." "I saw a dead bird on the way to school and it was really squashed." "I have new shoes on and they jump really high. Wanna see?" "My dad moved last night but I'm gonna visit him in his new apartment." I soon realized that if, as a teacher, I hoped to give knowledge back to the children, I would first have to be willing to receive it from them.

Because of their need to tell and do rather than listen, I discovered that the children also saw my role as teacher differently than I did. Although I was recognized as the 'in-charge person', the children eagerly assumed whatever control I would give them. I realized that, free from the traditional teacher-student roles, they preferred to see me as the moderator of their learning; I was allowed to design the environment, to help them make decisions whenever necessary, to answer the questions that were unanswerable by their peers, to mediate unsolvable arguments, and generally to provide the stability that an adult presence brings to any group of children. They were the controllers of their own learning; I was there when they needed me.

My realization of children's desire to be in control of their own learning was not acquired on my part without frustration, tears, and discarded lessons. However, in developing a better understanding of how children learn, I mastered my first real lesson in teaching—that, provided I gave them the chance, the children in my classroom could teach me more than I could ever hope to teach them. Armed with this knowledge, I set out to explore the kind of learning negotiated between teacher and students.

Understanding the World of Childhood

During this time, I also became intrigued by the differences between the world of childhood and my lived-in adult world. I envied those traits, common to many of the children, which were often carefully masked by adults: young children's openness with others; their curiosity about the unknown, and their desire to experiment with the untried; their sensitivity towards others in times of crisis; their willingness to speak their minds, possibly lacking the experience of the consequences, or perhaps unafraid of them; their uncanny ability to have an answer for everything based on the assumption that nothing is outside of their own experience; their belief that all problems are easily solved, and the concomitant expectation that the world is controllable through their own actions.

Indeed, the children in my classroom seemed to form an exclusive club to which adults could not belong—membership being determined by age, physical size, and limitation of experience. I was temporarily accepted into their world only because of my teacher-status. However, if I ever hoped to satisfy my innate curiosity about my young charges, I needed to find the means to understand more fully the world of childhood itself.

As a result of my observations, I began to spend considerable time sneaking around my classroom, seemingly preoccupied with adult tasks, while all the time spying on children's activities and eavesdropping on their conversations. I learned to value time spent 'kid-watching', observing the means by which children occupied themselves within learning situations, the ways in which they interacted with others, and their ability to solve problems in their own child-centred manner. I learned to take the time to listen to what children said to themselves as well as to their peers through the singsong monologue which often accompanied their play-work. I discovered that one means of learning more about how young children think was to question them about their own responses, although my queries were often met with stares of disbelief, not just because I dared to interfere with their tasks, but because they believed the answer was apparent to everyone. So it was that I learned that to become a teacher one must learn about both the children and the world they have created for themselves.

Thinking About the Importance of Gender

Comfortably ensconced in my role as 'kid-watcher', I soon began reflecting on how my views about gender were formed by the social influences of my own childhood. While growing up, my childhood playmates and elder role-models were happily female, participating in the pursuits that were traditionally viewed as acceptable for young girls: doll-play, dressing up, role-playing family situations (including fights over who had to play the father), and literacy activities. My pre-teen association with the boys in our community consisted of passively watching them participate in fishing, fort-building, war play, and games emphasizing strength and speed. I quickly learned to show incapability at their activities, becoming a supportive spectator and seldom questioning my right to participate. After all, these were boys' games and I was a girl.

From these childhood experiences, I learned that although boys and girls were expected to share the same space congenially, society maintained differing expectations for the behaviour of the two sexes, a view I carried with me through high school. I accepted my parents' expectation that I would seek higher education; however, my chosen career as a teacher was traditionally appropriate for females, and conformed to my underlying belief that women were valued most as domestic protectors of children and husbands.

Reflecting on my own genderedness as a child helped me to better understand the gendered behaviours I was observing within my own classroom. I began to wonder if, in spite of the fact that they are growing up in a technologically advanced society, young children continue to think, believe, and accept traditional roles for boys and girls, men and women—just as I did. Recent research on the gendered behaviours of children provided much support for my speculation.[1] It was the suspicion that children's perceptions of gender roles have not changed significantly in the past 30 years which prompted me to question the gender conceptions of the children I was teaching and observing in classrooms.

Realizing that the views of gender-appropriate behaviour I held as a child were enforced by the community in which I grew up, I began to wonder how the children in my classroom were influenced by the classroom community that I, the teacher, deliberately created. Was I allowing the world of school to become a miniature replication of the gendered practices I perceived to be prevalent in the larger society of which these children were a part? If, indeed, I could create a classroom sensitive to the effects of gender, would this be in conflict with the other influences that children face daily? I realized that it was time for me to explore systematically the gender influences within the classroom setting itself. By developing a better understanding of the way that children currently perceived gender, I hoped to be able to challenge their beliefs in a way that I was not challenged as a child.

Making Gender a Classroom Issue

I began, first of all, to explore ways to create a classroom environment that was deliberately sensitive to gender. Many of my efforts were trial and error, based on the ways the children respond-ed to the changes. I practised using terms like "snowpeople," as-sumed the Easter Bunny and the Tooth Fairy could be either male or female, and avoided phrases like "good girl" or "good boy" as rewards for behaviour. I spent more time observing and recording gendered play situations. I used both girls and boys to demonstrate new toys, and celebrated occasions when boys played in the house-centre or girls played with blocks or vehicles. I modified literature, songs, and games to allow equal representation of both sexes. I searched for books with girls and boys participating in non-conven-tional activities, books celebrating adventurous girls and nurturing boys, books about mothers and daughters together and fathers raising children. I deliberately initiated and recorded class discus-sions which I hoped would raise children's consciousness about gender issues, and then tried to figure out how the children arrived at their conclusions.

However, I soon came to the realization that what I was doing was just not enough. The children in my classroom were providing appropriate feedback on gender issues, but I was still searching for answers to questions which I considered essential to providing an educational environment that was truly sensitive to gender. For example, do young children recognize only the biological differ-ences between the two sexes or do they rely more heavily on social-ly-determined categories of behaviour for boys and girls? What major influences in children's lives contribute to their gendered-ness? Do children recognize a range of possibilities for their gen-der or do they view the categories as being strictly bipolar? How do children resolve the often conflicting messages about appro-priate gender behaviours presented by the home, school, and media?

As I was trying to decide how to find answers for these ques-tions, one of the children unintentionally provided a suggestion. During a discussion about boys and dolls, one boy turned to me in frustration and exclaimed, "You just don't understand about boys! You're a girl and so you know about girl things but you need to learn about boy things, too!" When I queried how I should do that, he replied, "That's simple. Just ask us. We know everything." I suddenly realized that this straightforward advice provided by a child might be the key to understanding. To discover a child's point of view, ask a child. It was at this point that I was determined to organize a formal research study focussing on children's conceptions of gender based on their interpretations of the gender roles they live daily. It was time also to take a close look at the research already undertaken on the issue.

Current Knowledge About School Children and Gender

An examination of the current research connecting gender and education supports my suspicion of the important role gender plays within educational programs. [A detailed discussion of recent research into gender and children may be found in Appendix B.] Not only are researchers concluding that boys and girls are being treated differently within the classroom setting, but it is becoming more widely acknowledged that girls are the ones who are suffering from the unequal treatment. As a result of the extension of societal stereotyping into our schools, girls are, as Spender & Sarah (1980, p. 27) so aptly put it, "learning how to lose" at the game of education, to be undemanding of teacher time, to remain passive background observers to boys' active learning, to view education through a male-biased curriculum, and to strive for success within traditional, domestic, nurturing careers—all behaviours reminiscent of my own schooling experience. Valuing gender-biased education requires of girls that they learn to accept their social inferiority, to reduce their personal expectations, and to lower their self-esteem. The end result is an education system which perpetuates the success of males at the expense of their female classmates.

However, much of the available research on the widespread stereotyping at work within the education system has focussed on older children, both with respect to the gender-based problems that children face within the classroom and the necessary interventions to rectify the inequities. Perhaps because of their lack of experiential knowledge, young children's understandings of gender have been largely ignored, except as interpreted by adults through observed play behaviours. Researchers seem hesitant to ask young

children to discuss their understanding of gender, to elaborate upon
the reasoning behind their ideas, and to trust that these responses
are meaningful to research. Since it is during these early childhood
years that attitudes and beliefs are formed and appropriate social
behaviours are reinforced,[2] there appears to be a need to look more
closely at how young children themselves view gender.

Furthermore, in spite of the fact that research points to the notion
that gender schemas are firmly based in the language we hear and
utilize, few studies explore the way in which the language that is
presented to young children within the classroom context contributes to their developing gender awareness. This seems surprising
in an educational system which relies on children's oral and written
language for the development and evaluation of literacy behaviours.[3] Since, in addition to being a communicative tool, language
functions as the means by which children learn to understand themselves as persons in relation to others in the social world, educational studies must re-examine not only the genderedness of the
language that is presented to children, but the ways in which children
themselves interpret and reproduce language. If, in fact, what
Davies (1989c, p. 1) says is true, that "in passing language on to
children we also pass on a relative entrapment in the social order,"
then additional studies to analyze the role that both expressive and
receptive language play in developing gender schema are necessary.

Although more researchers are now focussing on the role that
gendered language plays in forming children's beliefs about themselves,[4] few studies have examined the influence of the language of
children's literature, a surprising omission since many of the language programs used in schools today are ones that have replaced
traditional basal readers with an extensive literature collection. In
analyzing the influence of childhood reading materials on gender
perceptions, Segel (1986, p. 165) emphasizes the importance of
careful selection of children's literature "because the individual's
attitudes concerning appropriate gender-role behaviours are formed
during the early years," long before the reader has independent
choice of reading material. Thus it seems important that we examine children's responses to stories which contain sexual stereotypes, as well as their reactions to those which present non-conven-

tional gender behaviours. Research using the latter type, often referred to as "liberating" or "feminist" literature because it presents gender behaviours in non-conventional ways, shows that children typically resist literature which runs counter to their socialized gender beliefs.[5] It is the production of this resistance which researchers into gender find valuable because it is the challenging of children's value systems that creates the possibility of changing beliefs.

2 / Design of the Study

Responding to Stories as a Means of Understanding Gender

Children's responses to stories are indicative of their ongoing attempts to make sense of the world around them. With extensive exposure to fictional literature, they grow to understand and accept a world that is both fanciful and imaginary. At the same time, however, they are able to recognize the realistic elements embedded within the stories as they apply to their own lives. Thus, stories about real children and their families involved in potentially occurring situations help to forge a link between the fanciful world of storybook characters and the real world of the reader.[1]

Although in one sense it is their immediate experiences which assist children in making sense of an imaginary world, the reverse may also be true as the tale parallels their own lives and confirms their developing knowledge about the way in which real life operates. Favat[2] comments upon literature's ability to provide a sense of social order which children can generalize to their daily lives:

> Children's turning to the tale is no casual recreation or pleasant diversion; instead it is an insistent search for an ordered world more satisfying than the real one, a sober striving to deal with the crisis of experience they are undergoing....It would appear, moreover, that after reading a fairy tale, the reader invests the real world with the construct of the tale.

The end result is that continued exposure to stories not only helps children to develop an understanding of the differences and similarities between 'real' and 'pretend', but also provides them with an additional means of making sense of their own lives.

Although Davies (1989c) also acknowledges that fictional literature has an embedded moral order, she criticizes the gendered content of much of the literature to which children are exposed. By hearing stories that present characters in traditional gendered roles, not only do readers learn to recognize themselves as fitting acceptably into that environment, but they may become more critical when characters act in non-traditional ways.

> Stories provide the metaphors, the characters and the plots through which [children's] own positioning in the social world can be interpreted. Children's stories present them not only with the mundane gendered world of women in kitchens but also the fantasy world in which women escape kitchens and are beautiful and loved, their reward for which, is, of course, their own kitchen. If a woman is active and powerful she can only be accepted as such if her agency is directed in a selfless way towards a man or child whom she loves. Men, in contrast, have a much more complex array of possibilities—their power is admired and celebrated, their strength and cleverness can be associated with negative or positive powers, even both at the same time, and their right of access to safe domestic spaces by no means depends on their virtue. (p. 44)

Studies such as these suggest there is an inherent need not only to evaluate the types of literature to which children are being exposed in our schools, but as well to further explore children's responses to fictional literature that presents characters in non-conventional roles. The present study follows the latter course, using non-conventional literature as a viable, non-threatening means of accessing children's knowledge about gender. The stories selected provided the vehicle for discussion, presenting an unfamiliar world in which boys prefer dancing over sports and girls reject dolls in favour of climbing trees. The non-conventional positions presented within the story format are likely to be fanciful to children, while reality is represented by the underlying potential for real children to do these things successfully. The talk which evolves between researcher and child stems from the conflict between the imaginary world created within the story (explored through the researcher's questions) and the the real world from which the children draw experience.

The question remains as to whether or not these stories can have the desired effect on young readers. Because children have a tendency to resist change, sticking closely to that which is already familiar, stories presenting non-conventional behaviours are often disturbing to them. According to Zipes, who studied the effect of liberating fairy tales on children, this disturbance is necessary because it "interferes with the civilizing process in the hope of creating change." He implies that responses to discordant behaviours must be judged not by whether the new behaviours are accepted or rejected, but "on the unique ways they bring undesirable relations into question and force readers to question themselves."[3]

In her own study introducing non-conventional behaviours through feminist literature, Davies (1987) discusses the need to allow children the opportunity to build a conceptual framework that expands children's current understanding of gender.

> The central problem that children face in understanding and accepting non-traditional messages, is to know how a person (real or mythical) who acts outside of what is commonly understood as appropriate for their gender, can be recognized as expanding what is positively available to other like-gendered people. It is not enough that the model be there—i.e., that the non-conventional action be engaged in by a known person or known hero. It is essential that there is, as well, a conceptual framework which allows that person to be located not only as a positive member of his/her gender but to be seen to be behaving *appropriately* for that gender. (p. 43)

Thus, by discerning how children perceive the deviant actions of the characters, we are not only gaining insight into how they conceptualize gender, but may be encouraging them to question their own behaviours. Exposing the children to non-conventional behaviours and examining the ways in which they resist or accept the differences may be one means of confirming, broadening, and extending the conceptual framework children are developing about their own gendered behaviours.

Basic Assumptions

The study I finally undertook was based on several critical assumptions. The first one is that young children formulate perceptions of gender based on the culture in which they are immersed. These perceptions are formed through social interaction with family, school personnel and peers, and are strongly influenced through continued exposure to various forms of media, including the influence of children's literature. From these external influences, children learn that in order to be socially identified within their culture they must position themselves in a bipolar fashion as either a male or a female. Since acceptance into one of these categories is accompanied by specific social behaviours, girls and boys quickly adopt differing rules for appearance, speech patterns, movement, posture, and behavioural activities. It appears to be the social ordering of persons into bipolar categories which initiates the damaging sexual stereotyping practised by our society.[4]

I stated earlier that some theorists argue that gender is firmly rooted in the language base children develop through interacting with the world around them. From this evolved the second major assumption of this study: that children's developing conceptions of gender are expressed through the language that they use—more specifically, through their oral responses to literature. It appears that language and gender form a two-way street; children not only develop an understanding of gender through the language that they receive from others but, in turn, express their learned gender conceptions through the language that they produce. Studies by Davies and Zipes[5] show that this cyclic language-gender pattern is disrupted when the language received is in conflict with the children's understanding of gender, as is the case when literature which portrays non-conventional gender behaviours is used to challenge traditional beliefs.

The final assumption of the study is that children are naturally active constructors of knowledge whose perceptions of gender can undergo change.[6] Although their lack of experience may cause the perspective from which they observe events to be different than an adult view, because children are involved in the process of seeking out new information, we need to pay attention to their beliefs and the means by which they are constructed, deconstructed, and reconstructed.

Since children's understanding of gender is still in the formative stage, research on gender perceptions is complicated by the effects of the numerous external influences that they encounter. Children between the ages of 4 and 8 are busily occupied confirming their developing gender identities by categorizing behaviours as appropriate for 'boys-only', 'girls-only', or 'boys and girls'. At the same time, teachers, parents, peers, and the media are bombarding children with images, often conflicting, of the differing ways that boys and girls are expected to behave in order to learn socially acceptable gender roles. The end result is that although children within this age range seem to be becoming aware of the differences between their own gender identities and the gender roles they are expected to fulfil, their responses will naturally reveal the inconsistency of their understanding.

It follows, then, that a study which focusses on the ways that children express gender through their responses to literature in a primary-school classroom may give the researcher a better understanding of how young children perceive gender. By determining what the children already know about gender from previous experiences and by observing how this knowledge is revealed through their responses within the classroom environment—particularly when the literature that has been selected portrays non-conventional gender roles—we can then make predictions about the design of future school programs to facilitate a broadening of children's understanding of gender.

Methodology

More and more educational research is qualitative in nature,[7] occurring within the actual school settings that will benefit from the knowledge gained. Here the classroom teacher becomes the researcher, describing and interpreting observable recurring patterns of behaviours. This form of research, which allows for the wider context in which educational programs function, is based in the reality of the school culture.[8] The methodology selected for this study relied on observations made within the classroom context. Furthermore, because young children are such highly reactive subjects with attitudes and temperaments which may be affected by exposure to unfamiliar situations, consistent routines and familiar personnel were maintained throughout the collection of the data. In fact, an emergent study such as this one, carried out by a familiar teacher/researcher within the classroom environment, should increase the probability of consistent behaviours. Details about the application of the methodology will by given as we go along.

The Subjects

Observations for this study took place between the months of January and April in a school located in an urban area of a city in southwestern Ontario. The children participating included those enrolled in a half-day Junior Kindergarten program, a half-day Senior Kindergarten program, and a full-day Grade One program. Different grade levels were selected in an attempt to observe gender conceptions of children at varying ages. Classrooms were chosen based on their physical proximity to each other within the school setting, and the willingness of the three participating teachers to involve their children in the study.

A total of 18 participants were involved: three girls and three boys from each classroom, ranging in age from four years, three months to six years, nine months when the study began. The children were selected by the classroom teachers, in consultation with the researcher, based on two criteria observed during the regular language program: the ability to articulate views and opinions orally during classroom discussions, and the ability to listen and respond to literature written specifically for children. In cases where more than six children in each class were able to meet both of the criteria, the final selections were made randomly. It should be noted that the sample represented a range of cultural and class differences, a reflection of the school population itself.

My choice of language-based criteria to select the children meant that their backgrounds were diverse, a factor which probably influenced the way in which they perceived the gender-related issues. Although I did not deliberately set out to explore each family situation, I knew from teacher-parent discussions that some children came from home environments which modelled and rewarded specific and separate roles for males and females, while others were from family backgrounds in which parents attempted to ensure that boys and girls were raised with the same expectations for behaviour and accomplishments. The depiction of the different ways in which the children *perceive* gender and grapple with its inconsistencies, rather than what *causes* the differences, is the principal focus of this study. My method will be descriptive and analytical.

The Classroom Contexts

Because the study relied on children's understanding and utilization of language, a description of the classroom contexts, representative of the teachers' approaches to language learning, is necessary.

All three classroom environments were designed to support the belief that children need opportunities to 'play with literacy' in order to learn more about reading and writing. Thus, although the usual kinds of play equipment were evident (manipulative toys, sand, water, paints, puzzles, etc.), materials supportive of reading and writing were also present and easily accessed. A variety of books was on prominent display in the classrooms and widely used throughout the day. The writing centres were filled with markers, pens, pencils, and assorted types of paper and booklets, and occupied a central portion of each room. Overall, a reading/writing climate was predominant and illustrated by the child-made signs defining classroom rules and routines, by the ready access to pencils and paper at a variety of centres, and by the children busily occupied with making reading and writing a regular part of their day.

The daily programs in all three rooms were also organized within a literacy orientation. In the Junior and Senior Kindergarten programs, the day began with an informal book time when children listened to and read an assortment of literature with volunteers and teachers. Circle-time provided opportunities for shared reading, for response to quality literature, and for teacher and child-recorded print—along with the usual songs, games, and finger-plays. Three or four times a week at the end of the day, a regularly scheduled writing time occurred when all of the children wrote together at tables.

In the Grade One program, a large block of the day was devoted to the integration of reading, writing, and other language activities. The language program here was similar to the one offered in Kindergarten, with additional time spent on shared reading and writing, the acquisition of individual skills, and productive group work. At least one-quarter of the day was devoted to writing, including an emphasis on idea generation, patterning, rough drafts, and publication of a finished product. The children were also free to choose writing as an activity during centre-time.

Description of the Literature-Response Sessions

The literature-response sessions, used to initiate the gender-related discussions with the children and provide the primary data for observation and analysis, were organized in the following manner.

Each child participated individually in four literature-response sessions over a 12-week time period. During each session, I briefly introduced the book to be read on that day, allowed time for the child to examine it, and then read it aloud. Throughout the sessions, the children were encouraged to ask questions about anything they did not understand. The children were then asked a series of pre-selected questions (included in Appendix A and described below), both to determine their understanding of the way that gender was portrayed in the story and to elicit discussion about their own beliefs about gender. Each session was audio-taped, and the children's responses were transcribed for analysis at a later date. Prior to the discussion sessions, the children were given opportunities to experiment with the mini-recorder and hear themselves on tape. The amount of time spent on each session depended on the length of the book and the child's attention, generally between 20 and 30 minutes.

It should be noted that the portion of the study examining the children's responses to literature did not interfere with regular classroom programming. The children were already accustomed to conferencing with their classroom teachers about literature selections; they now had the opportunity to conference individually with a different adult, one with whom they were already familiar.[9]

Selecting the Literature to Promote Discussion

Selection of the four literature choices was not an easy task. Whereas there is a plethora of literature available for young children, very few choices present characters engaging in behaviours which were felt to cause children to question their own gender beliefs. The final four choices, selected from a wide variety of children's literature, were based on the following criteria:

1. The books were attractively presented and illustrated so as to engage children's interest.
2. They were recommended as being suitable for four-to-seven-year-olds by a publication which promotes non-sexist children's literature.[10]
3. The story action focussed on a single, human character although other characters were present in secondary roles. For two of the choices, the main character was male and for the other two, female.
4. The main character behaved in some way that was at odds with conventional gender roles; for example, male children preferred to dance or play dress up, whereas female children preferred active roles which required strength and cleverness. To determine what behaviours children considered non-conventional, 30 children outside of this study, between the ages of four and seven, were asked to define gendered behaviours they found to be unacceptable for girls or for boys. Only those books portraying one or more of these behaviours were included in the final selection.
5. In each of the four books, the main character was criticized by parents or peers for non-conventional behaviour, although, at the story's conclusion, the problem was resolved in a positive manner.
6. Based on my own teaching experience, the books were considered suitable for generating discussions upon which the children's understanding of gender could be elaborated.

In order for the reader to gain an understanding of the author's intended message within each story, detailed descriptions of the four selections follow, in the sequence in which they were presented to the children. A brief overview of the children's initial conception of each book has also been included.

1. Robert Munsch (1980) *The Paper Bag Princess*

The book begins in usual fairy tale fashion, as the beautiful Princess Elizabeth plans to marry the handsome Prince Ronald. However, plans are interrupted as a fire-breathing dragon destroys the Kingdom and spirits Prince Ronald off to his cave. Elizabeth, messy, charred, and dressed only in a paper bag, sets out to rescue her Prince, and bravely tricks the dragon into falling asleep. As the impeccably suited Ronald finally stands before her, still swinging his tennis racquet, he tells her, "Boy, are you a mess! You smell like ashes, your hair is all tangled and you are wearing a dirty old paper bag. Come back when you are dressed like a real princess" (p. 21). Elizabeth retorts, "Ronald, your clothes are really pretty and your hair is all neat. You look like a real prince, but you are a bum" (p. 23). As Elizabeth dances her way into the sunset, still dressed in her paper bag, the reader is told that they did not get married after all.

Of the four stories used in this study, responses to this one were the most difficult to interpret, not only because the fairy-tale format is less based in reality, but also because the story line simultaneously transforms both male and female roles. The intent of this story is to present a successful instance of role reversal wherein a female hero, independent, intelligent, brave and capable, rescues her knight in shining armour. In casting the female as the controlling agent, both the dragon and the prince are intended, by contrast, to appear as vain, weak, unintelligent, and somewhat foolish. The reader is left with the suggestion that the familiar fairy-tale ending, where the prince and princess live happily ever after, is not the only acceptable road to happiness. However, although these messages are clear to most adults, the children in the study varied in their understanding of the intent of the characters, based on the children's developing expectations that males and females should act differently.

2. Tomie de Paola (1979) *Oliver Button Is a Sissy*

The intent of the storyline in *Oliver Button Is a Sissy* is to show that it is important for children to pursue the things they like, even in the face of opposition. In Oliver's case, the conflict arises with his pursuit of play activities which would traditionally be considered as feminine, and therefore unacceptable socially. Early in the story, the reader is told that Oliver does not like to do the things that boys are supposed to do, preferring to walk in the woods, skip, read books, and play dress-up. Although these pursuits are never directly identified as 'girl things', this is implied by Oliver's father who suggests that any boy not interested in sports is "a sissy." In need of exercise, Oliver enrols in dancing class. The label "sissy" is further reinforced by Oliver's peer group when the boys write "Oliver Button is a sissy" on the school wall. As the story progresses, Oliver, unsuccessful at what are conventionally accepted as male pursuits, becomes an accomplished tap dancer, participating in a talent show which many of his classmates attend. Although he does not win the contest (a fact disappointing to most children), his father accepts and rewards his new-found talent and the boys at school change the sign on the wall to read "Oliver Button is a star."

The children had some difficulty interpreting the author's intent within this story as some children felt that either the teacher, Oliver's parents, or the girls had changed the writing on the wall at the story's conclusion. As a result, those children who failed to understand that the boys now accepted Oliver's dancing, felt that he should stop dancing and return to more boyish pursuits.

3. Bruce Mack (1979) *Jesse's Dream Skirt*

The intent of this story is to encourage young children to question certain physical attributes associated with girls and boys, in this case, clothing. As the story begins, Jesse is introduced as a preschool-aged boy who enjoys dressing up in his mother's old clothes. One night, he dreams of a multi-coloured skirt that "whirled, twirled, flowed and glowed and felt soft inside" (p. 8), and excitedly tells his mother about his dream. She offers to make it for him, after warning him that the other children might make fun of him. When the skirt is finally finished, Jesse wears it to preschool. Although his teacher tells him that he likes it, the other children call Jesse a "sissy," making fun of him until he runs off crying. In an attempt to resolve the problem, the teacher calls a classroom discussion in which the children voice varying opinions about why Jesse should or should not be able to wear a skirt. One boy tells about an incident where his father yelled at him for dressing up in his mother's clothes, while a girl relates how it feels to be teased about wearing a baseball uniform. At the story's conclusion, the teacher brings in a box of material which the children use to make skirts, capes, ribbons, and turbans, dancing and shouting around the room. The reader is left with the impression that the children have become more accepting of Jesse's skirt, with some even feeling that the choice of clothing should be left up to the child.

Although most of the children in this study understood the author's intended message, in general, a boy wearing a skirt was considered such extreme behaviour that they had difficulty conceptualizing its being chosen at all. As a result, many of the children, particularly the boys, clung tenuously to their belief that Jesse had made a mistake which he would now be able to correct.

4. Miriam Schlein (1975) *The Girl Who Would Rather Climb Trees*

The final book presented to the children seemed the simplest in story line and the most easily understood by the children. The main character, Melissa, is what the author describes as "an all-around girl" (p. 11), enjoying a variety of activities, including several pursuits which most children associate more with boys than with girls. One day Melissa's mother brings her home a large doll, complete with frilly clothing, and an elaborate carriage. Melissa, however, does not know how to play with the doll and has to be shown what to do successively by her mother, her grandmother, and her mother's best friend, who are pictured drinking tea in the kitchen. Not really liking the doll because it doesn't do anything, Melissa soon solves her problem by putting the doll to sleep and going outside to return to her favourite pursuit, climbing trees.

The author's intent is to suggest that there is value for both boys and girls in participating in a variety of activities, with the underlying subtext being that all girls need not like to do traditional 'girl things'. Most children understood part of this message, allowing that since Melissa did not really like the doll, she should not have to play with it. However, because many of the children remained convinced that all girls should like dolls and would therefore want to play with them, they attributed Melissa's behaviour to the unsuitability of this particular doll. As a result, most children concluded that Melissa could continue to do other things but should find another doll, one that she would like.

Establishing the Questions

The introductory questions were common to all four stories and designed not only to relax the children, but to encourage them to talk about their understanding of the story. (See Appendix A for a list of all pre-selected questions.) "Did you like this story?" "What was your favourite part?" represent the type of question designed to find out whether or not the children understood the story's meaning. These were followed by questions specific to each story, formulated to encourage children to talk about the non-conventional behaviours of the characters. Questions such as "What do you think it means to be a sissy?," "Do you think that Jesse should have worn his skirt to school?," and "Was it okay for Ronald to tell Elizabeth that she looked a mess?" explored the children's understanding of the characters' behaviours associated with gender.

Other questions encouraged the children to put themselves in the place of the storybook characters, in order to determine how they themselves would respond in a similar situation; for example, "If you woke up one day and found your clothes burned off and your friends kidnapped by a dragon, what would you do?," "What would you do if you were Oliver and everyone made fun of you for being different?," "Would you like it if someone gave you a present like Melissa's doll? What would you do with it?"

Another set of questions asked the children to make judgements about gender issues based on their own beliefs: "Why do you think that girls are allowed to wear pants but boys can't wear skirts? Is that fair?," "Do you think that a doll would be a good present for a girl? Would a doll be a good present for a boy?," "Do you think this is a girl dragon or a boy dragon or do you know?" Related questions explored children's beliefs about their own gendered behaviours: "Are most of your friends boys or girls or both boys and girls?," "What are your favourite things to play with?," "What clothes do you like to wear to school?"

At the end of each session, the children were asked to comment on the story's conclusion—whether or not they liked the ending, how it made them feel, and whether they would change it in any way.

It was not possible, nor was it necessary, within the time allotted to ask each child every single question; had I tested the children's patience to that degree, I might never have enticed them back for a second story. Instead, the questions selected encouraged the children to discuss those gender issues that seemed important to *them*. Their concerns were easily recognized as they returned again and again to the part of the story that most interested them.

It should be noted that when the children were initially invited to participate, the purpose of the study was described to them as "a way of finding out what children like you think about books like these." Throughout the sessions, although the children's responses were guided and extended by the questions, I tried to make it clear that there were no right answers and that their own thoughts and ideas were important. I frequently used phrases such as, "I can't figure this out. Maybe you can help me" or "I don't know the answer to this but maybe you do" to introduce the questions, and provided continuous positive reinforcement for their answers.

Researcher Bias

During my analysis of the data, I came to realize that, by necessity, my own values were implicit in my interpretation of the responses provided by the children. Patton supports this notion when he says that what people 'see' in the data is highly dependent on their backgrounds: "Our culture tells us what to see; our early childhood socialization instructs us how to look at the world; and our value system tells us how to interpret what passes before our eyes."[11] Initially, this realization worried me, since I feared my analysis would be overly biased by the personal notions and expectations about gender that I presently hold. I recognize that as a teacher I am influenced by my intimate knowledge of the children's personalities, behaviours, and family backgrounds. As a woman, I have knowledge of the power that males hold over females in our society and may inadvertently judge children's answers as indicators of how they will grow to view personal relationships. As an adult, I understand that children's conceptions of the world are far more limited than mine, and that their views will necessarily change and adapt over time as they grow older and gain life experience and knowledge. All of these influences may have unintentionally affected my interpretation of the data. However, every attempt has been made to provide enough data—the children's actual words in conversation—and to link my own conclusions with corroborative studies to allow readers to make up their own minds.

Moreover, since the knowledge I bring to the interpretation of the children's responses is a result of my continued involvement with children and the society in which they live, it needs to be recognized as a valued part of the research process. Further, I have tried throughout to practise what Patton refers to as disciplined observational methods: "learning how to write descriptively, practising the disciplined recording of field notes, [and] knowing how to separate detail from trivia."[12]

As a teacher/researcher, then, I acknowledge that I have been selective in the data that I have chosen to value, as well as in the personal interpretations and meanings I have assigned to the children's words. Although I believe that I have interpreted their responses as the children intended them, I realize that what I have included and what I have left out reflect both my personal choices and range of experience. It is possible that another researcher, relying on a somewhat different knowledge base and experience, would view the data differently, culling alternative themes from the children's responses.

Analysis of Observations

At the end of each day's sessions, I transcribed the data recorded on the audio-tapes, adding any field notes I had taken about the children's responsive behaviours. Although transcribing this amount of data was a voluminous task, I found the process to be beneficial because I heard the data once again through the children's own voices, and was able to note any emphasis or inflection that would make the data more meaningful. As the study progressed, I learned how to encourage the children to expand their answers and allowed them increased talking time without interference. As the children accepted that we were engaged in reciprocal learning, they also became more confident and lengthened their responses. Together we learned to relax and enjoy the sessions.[13]

Because each of the subjects was responding to the same book during this initial transcription process, I was able to see patterns and themes beginning to emerge. I began to note recurrent themes, and to search for them in the responses to the remaining stories. I then made a list of what I felt were the most prevalent themes and cross-referenced them with supporting examples from the children's responses.

Although I had initially arranged the themes according to the literature selection which prompted them, I soon realized that several of the themes were being duplicated. So I began to search for common themes across all four stories and to note which ones appeared only in response to one or two of the selections. At the same time, I was paying attention to the similarities and differences between boys and girls and to both groups at different ages. Once I was certain that the themes I had chosen to describe were, in my judgment, the most evident from the data, I attempted to correlate these trends with similar gender studies of young children. Four themes, with several interesting subthemes, emerged: the reliance on visible markers to define gender, play behaviours ('girl things' versus 'boy things'), social relationships, and rules (the assignment of control). These are the focus of the next two chapters.

3 / Visible Markers and Play Behaviours

Although there is always some confusion when distinguishing between the terms 'sex' and 'gender' (since both terms are often construed as social categories) in this book 'sex' will be used to denote the biological differences between males and females, while 'gender' will refer to the social differences between the sexes (designated by the terms girl and boy, woman and man, or masculine and feminine). Hence, 'gender role' will refer here to the learned social behaviours that children associate with either being a boy or being a girl.

Reliance on Visible Markers to Define Gender

Research on play behaviours suggests that young children rely heavily on visible markers to indicate maleness or femaleness, basing their judgements on hair length, the presence or absence of hair adornments, clothing, jewellery, and make-up. Minimal attention is paid to genital differences, probably because society teaches children at a very young age that genitalia are to be kept secret and hidden, and not talked about publicly. Behavioural differences are less apparent to young children and act as a secondary source of information.[1] A situation that occurred in my classroom during a play session illustrates how easily children are able to ignore biological differences in the face of visible characteristics which they have classified as being associated with either boys or girls. Two four-year-old girls were pretending to bathe their "babies" in the house-centre, with Katie holding a girl doll while Jill held a boy doll. Both dolls were anatomically correct and were unclothed at the time. The boy doll, having a slightly darker skin tone, had lips that were pinkish in colour.

KATIE: I'm giving my daughter a bath.
JILL: Well, I'm giving my daughter a bath, too.
KATIE: That can't be a daughter. That's a boy, not a girl.
JILL: She is not. Can't you see her lipstick?
KATIE: Look! That's a boy (*points to genitals*).
JILL: Well, don't you know that boys don't wear lipstick?
KATIE: I guess you're right. We both have girls.

In spite of previous exposure to genital differences, both children relied more heavily on the use of make-up as an indicator of the sex of the baby.

This reliance on visible physical attributes is evident throughout the stories as children repeatedly noted how the physical characteristics of the storybook characters suggest maleness or femaleness. In *The Paper Bag Princess*, for instance, in spite of the fact that the story was read making the sex of the dragon neutral (the actual script identifies it as a male), all of the children in the study stated that the dragon was "a boy." These findings are in agreement with a study by Intons-Peterson which found that when labelling figures whose hair length was concealed (or in the dragon's case, non-existent), as either male or female, the absence of female-associated hair characteristics increased the likelihood that the character would be called a boy.[2] Kessler and McKenna also found a societal bias toward making a male gender attribution about nondescript figures. It seems that with both children and adults, "male characteristics are construed as more obvious."[3]

Although it is possible that several of the children may have been exposed to this story at home or during earlier school experiences, when asked how they knew that the dragon was male, none of the children referred to the pronoun 'he'. Instead, many of the children's responses appeared to result from their own beliefs about male-associated physical attributes—including colouring, length of tail, antennae, type of points on its back, voice, and absence of eyelashes.

Is this a girl dragon or a boy dragon?
I think it's a boy because boys have green where other dragons have red. See here on their antennae. And boys have just a few of those red bumps and the girls would have lots.
Anything else?
Let me see. White. See white birds look like girls and this dragon isn't white. Only kinda white like there, on its stomach.
Brent / 4

It's a boy 'cause he has wings and just boys have wings. And these sharp claws. Boys need those for fighting.
Do girl dragons fight, too?
No, they'll just stand back and let this daddy one do it for them.
Ann / 4

I just think it's a boy because his stomach don't look like a girl's.
How would a boy's stomach look?
Fat and chubby.   *Paul / 5*

When asked to elaborate further, John did his best to describe the dragon's male mannerisms.

Well, boys stand like that with their feet and lean on things. And sometimes boys cross their legs like this and put their feet up on things.   *John / 6*

Several children had difficulty explaining themselves, commenting that the dragon "just looked like a boy."

It just looks like a boy...because it's uglier.
Do you think boy dragons are uglier than girl dragons?
I think they're both the same but this one just looks like a boy...kinda.   *Dawn / 6*

It appears as if, based on their socialized need to fit everyone into one of the two categories, children gain a sense of whether a character is male or female. The physical characteristics provide the initial cues about categorization because they are visible, familiar, and easily classified within the children's experiences.

Similarly, children relied on external physical characteristics to confirm that human characters were either girls or boys. In *Jesse's Dream Skirt*, when Dawn dressed up in a baseball uniform, it was acceptable to most children because the physical markers designating her as a girl, long hair and barrettes, were still visible.

> **Do you think that Dawn looks like a boy when she wears that uniform?**
> No, because she's a girl.
> **How do you know she's a girl?**
> Because she doesn't want to be a boy. Look at her long hair. Boys don't wear long hair...girls do. So she wants to be a girl.
> *Jill / 4*
>
> I can see her long eyelashes so she's a girl. And her has got soft skin. And it looks like her has powder on. So her must be a girl.
> *Brent / 4*

However, because both boys and girls can have short hair, when Jesse wore a skirt it became too difficult for some children to identify him as either a girl or a boy.

> **How do you think Jesse looks in that skirt?**
> Not good.
> **Why do you say that?**
> It makes him look like a girl. See he just has short hair so you can't tell so good. But he doesn't have earrings on so that helps us know.   *John / 6*

It appears that the correct assigning of biological sex only becomes a problem when the individual no longer has recognizable traits designating maleness or femaleness, particularly if hair and clothing cues provide mixed messages. In Jesse's case, the children became uncomfortable because, although informed within the story that he was a boy, his clothing indicated differently.

The need to label people clearly as one sex or the other is also apparent in children's association of colours with specific sexes. When asked if certain colours were for boys or for girls, most responded that although boys and girls could wear any colours they wanted, certain colours were clearly designated as boys' colours or girls' colours. With very few exceptions, children responded that black, brown, blue, and green were considered boys' colours while pink, red, orange, and yellow were girls' colours. Fluorescent colours and purple were considered neutral.

> **Do you think that there are certain colours for boys and girls?**
> Yes. Well, no. Boys can wear pink and other girls' colours and girls can wear boys' colours. It's okay.
> **So what do you think are girls' colours?**
> Pink and red and yellow.
> **And what do you think are boys' colours?**
> Brown, black, and blue.
> **Do girls ever talk about boys' colours and girls' colours?**
> No. We just know what we should wear 'cause we're girls.
> *Meri / 6*

When examining the main colours of children's clothing today, it is not surprising that children hold this impression. Colours are even being used by toy manufacturers to suggest to the consumer that certain toys are more acceptable for one sex or the other; in the words of Carlsson-Paige & Levin: "whereas the current lines of toys for girls appear in mute pastel colours—primarily lavender and pink, the bolder greens, blues, and blacks are reserved for the boys."[4] It is more surprising, however, that although the children clearly assigned colours to each sex, many of them felt it was acceptable for boys to wear girls' colours and vice versa.

> **Are there any special colours that only boys should wear?**
> Black and brown. That's really boys' colours. But boys could wear pink sometimes. Girls wear it mostly but boys could wear it, too. But, well...all of the colours is for boys and girls really. Even black as long as girls know.
> **Know what?**
> Know that they're wearing boys' colours. Then it's okay.
> *Jason / 6*

It seems that as their understanding increases, children come to realize that the colour of their clothing does not need to be the ultimate determinant of whether they are a girl or a boy.

One of the discussions that arose within this study dealt with what happens when these visible markers—acceptably categorized as appropriate for males, females, or both—disguise or provide misinformation about the wearer's sex. This occurred in *Jesse's Dream Skirt* when Jesse wore a skirt to school. Although most children responded negatively to Jesse's skirt, saying that he looked funny in it and resembled a girl, there was a wide range of responses regarding the acceptability of his behaviour. Responses ranged from outright denial that he would be allowed to wear it, to agreement that, although he technically would be able to wear it, he should not do so. The children's rationale for their lack of acceptance was that transgression of the 'skirts are for girls' rule would result in undesirable consequences. Not only would Jesse be socially ostracized since everyone would laugh and make fun of him, but someone in control, a parent, teacher, or principal, would subsequently become angry and he would be punished.

> **If Jesse wears his skirt to school, what do you think the other children will say?**
> They'll say, "Jesse, you look ridiculous."
> **And what about the teacher?**
> Probably he'll say, "Go right home and take that off this instant. You look ridiculous," and then he'll send him to the principal's office. *Ann / 4*

> **What would the teacher say if one of the boys in your class wore a skirt to school?**
> She'd say (*shouts*), "You take that skirt off and go right back home! Now!" *Jimmy / 5*

Since Jesse portrays a male character with which the boys hope to identify, it is not surprising that their responses are more negative than the girls, with less room for discussion. When asked whether or not they would ever wear a skirt to school, several of the boys were shocked at the suggestion.

> **Do you think it's a good idea for a boy to wear a skirt to school?**
> No way! No way! Aargh...girls! Girls only! I will never, ever

wear a skirt in my whole life!   *Brent / 4*

If you think that boys would ever want to wear skirts then you just don't know about boys!   *John / 6*

Although two of the boys did confide that they sometimes dressed up in their sisters' skirts at home, they stated that they would never wear one to school. It seemed that the girls were more tolerant of clothing variances and more willing to let Jesse try wearing a skirt, either because they did not have to identify with Jesse's non-conventional behaviour because he was male, or perhaps because many of them enjoyed the experience of wearing skirts.

What would you do if a boy in your class wore a skirt to school?
I'd just ignore him or say, "You look nice in that."
So you wouldn't mind if a boy wore a skirt to school?
No. Kids should wear what they want.   *Meri / 6*

How do you think Jesse looks in that skirt?
Well, at first I didn't really like him in it, but now I kinda do.
Would it be okay if a boy in your class wore a skirt to school?
Yeah, if he wanted. I wouldn't care. He should just wear what he wants.   *Cathy / 6*

It thus becomes apparent that displaying appropriate visible markers is important to children as one means of helping them decide whether an individual is male or female. It is when these physical markers disguise or provide misinformation about the sex of the wearer that discomfort arises.

Play Behaviours: 'Boy Things' Versus 'Girl Things'

A second recurrent theme evident through the children's responses was their need to define certain play behaviours as being traditionally associated with boys or with girls. These responses were most evident following a reading of two stories, *Oliver Button Is a Sissy* and *The Girl Who Would Rather Climb Trees*.

In response to these stories, the children defined toys, games, and sports appropriate for boys and girls, as well as the play behaviours that accompany these activities. They also identified several neutral activities in which both boys and girls may participate without fear of recrimination. As with their division of colours according to the sex that should wear them, the children pointed out that girls were 'allowed' to play 'boy things' and vice versa under specific conditions.

In general, skipping, dressing up, playing with dolls, picking flowers, and dancing were behaviours identified by the children as suitable for girls, while boys were expected to participate in football, baseball, basketball, soccer, hockey, karate, and fighting.

What are some things that you think boys like to do?
Play football and baseball and hockey, which I do with my friends. Go biking. More boys do that than girls. Do fighting and rough stuff like that.
Can girls do those things, too?
Well...I guess they could. But most of them don't.
Why not?
I guess they don't want to. Some girls might do those things. *Jason / 6*

Are there any things that you think are just for girls?
Well, dancing, like in the book, and skipping, although boys can do that. They just don't want to do it much.
Anything else?
Well, I guess, dressing up and playing with their dolls because that's what girls do a lot.   *Matt / 6*

Can you think of any games that are mostly for boys or mostly for girls?
Well girls like hopscotch and Barbies and stuff like that. Boys like...well, they like fighting and karate. And boys play games where they get all covered in mud, like football.
Do you like to do those things?
Some girls might, but I don't.   *Mandy / 4*

In most cases, reading books and drawing pictures could be safely enjoyed by both girls and boys although several children pointed out that girls spend more time with these activities.

Can you think of any things that both boys and girls do?
Well we can both do things at school like painting and drawing and writing books.
Do both boys and girls in your class do those things?
Yeah. But I think girls might do them more. Girls paint more and draw pictures and colour and do crafts. But the boys make funnier things. *Leann / 5*

What kinds of things do you think both boys and girls do?
Both of us can make things, like out of paper. And both of us can read books.
Do you like to read books?
Yeah. But I like Ninja Turtles better. I have a Ninja colouring book.
What kinds of books do girls like?
Oh...probably books about Barbies and cats and dogs.
Jimmy / 5

While dolls were repeatedly designated as 'girl toys', boys were perceived as playing with trucks, trains, racing cars, dinky toys, blocks, plastic animals (provided they portrayed a 'tough' nature such as lions, bulls, or gorillas), and superhero figures such as Ninja Turtles, GI Joe, He-Man, and Batman.

What toys do you like to play with?
Oh, I like blocks and the tow truck and the dump truck. And the animals. But just the tough animals.
What animals are "tough?"
The lion and the bull and the gorilla.
Do girls play with the animals?
Yeah. But they only play with the sheep and the cow and the goat and the chickens 'cause the boys get the rest. *Jimmy / 5*

What toys do girls like to play with?
Girls like dolls and playing house and talking on the phone.
Do boys do that?
Not as much. Boys like to do cars and trucks and blocks better.
Can girls play with cars and trucks, too?
Yeah. If they want. But they know those are boy toys.
Ann / 4

A closer examination of the lists of 'boy things' and 'girl things' as identified by the children throughout the study reveals that the boys enjoy a far wider range of acceptable behaviours through their toy selections, games, and sports activities. Even the social positionings allowed for boys encourage more freedom. The children expected boys to be physically active, to spend more time out of doors or at each other's houses, to be rougher and engage in 'play fighting', to run a lot, to play noisily, and to voice their opinions. Contrasting verbal descriptions of how girls should play suggested that children believe girls spend more time indoors, play more quietly with toys, are more involved in fantasy play, and more passive in their manner, actions, and speech.

> Well, my brother is a boy so he's bigger and rougher than me. He runs a lot.
> **Does your brother do the same things as you?**
> No. He likes to visit his friends and do fighting and things. I don't do that.
> **What do you like to do that's different?**
> Well, I usually just walk and not run, or I stay inside and play dolls with my friends. *Leann / 5*

> **How do you think boys and girls play differently?**
> Well, boys like to be outside climbing trees all the time. Me and my brother build forts and shoot people and play guns and things.
> **Do girls do those things?**
> No, my sister mostly stays home with her friends and has tea parties. *Travis / 6*

These generalized descriptions of expected behaviours show that the children have very different impressions about expected and allowable behaviours for boys and for girls. It is these differing conceptions children hold of how boys and girls are expected to behave which I set out to examine by asking questions, listening to opinions, and discussing alternatives.

Early in the discussions with the children it became evident that children distinguish which activities are appropriate for boys and which are appropriate for girls. Furthermore, from their conversations, it became apparent that one could codify a set of tacit rules established in the world of childhood that provide children with the information needed to cope socially. These rules—embedded in their responses—are given below (in no specific order).

Children's Rules About 'Boy Things' and 'Girl Things'

RULE 1: Toys, games, sports, and play activities are categorized as being either 'for girls only', 'for boys only', or 'neutral—for everyone'.

> **Tell me some things that you think boys do.**
> Football and dinky cars and playing GI Joes.
> **Why do you think boys do those things?**
> Because they're boys' stuff. They're supposed to like them. That's the rule—for boys only. The boys I know always do play with them.
> **Are there rules for girls, too?**
> Yeah, the rule says that girls are supposed to play with dolls instead of trucks. *Jill / 4*
>
> **Are there any things that both boys and girls can do?**
> Boys can do whatever things are okay for boys to do and girls do what's okay for girls to do.
> **How do you know what's okay?**
> You can just ask your friends or watch what they do. *John / 6*

RULE 2: Neutral toys and activities are equally available to both sexes and include activities such as reading books, drawing pictures, painting, playing in sand and water, swimming, gymnastics, using the climbers, going to the beach, and participating in games such as hide-and-go-seek.

> **Are there things that you do that girls can do, too?**
> I go swimming and girls can go swimming, too.
> **Anything else?**
> Sometimes karate. There are a few girls in my karate class but not many. Some girls do gymnastics and boys do that, too.

What about things in our classroom?
Boys and girls can both read books. And paint pictures and make
things, too.   *Bryan / 4*

RULE 3:   Boys can participate in girls' activities or play with girls'
toys under the following conditions:

- They play with them privately (that is, at home).
- They know that they are playing with girls' toys or activities and
  verbalize that knowledge.
- They play with them with a peer group and everyone in the group
  agrees to play.
- They are instructed to play with them by an adult and therefore
  are "allowed."
- If teased or ridiculed, they immediately stop playing and select
  suitable boys' activities.

Was it okay for Oliver to keep on dancing?
No, because that's a girl thing. He's a boy.
Can boys ever do girl things?
Only if their moms and dads say it's okay.
**So if Oliver's dad said he could keep on dancing, then it was
okay for him to do a girl thing?**
Yeah. But his friends might laugh.   *Bryan / 4*

Do you ever dress up in skirts and twirl around?
Sometimes at home I try on my sister's skirt.
Would you ever wear it to school?
No way. My friends would laugh at me.   *Travis / 6*

Would you ever play girl things?
Maybe if my friends did, too. Like if all the boys play with the
dolls in the house-centre. Then it's okay.
What if some of your friends made fun of you?
I'd just give the doll to a girl and go play with the boys again.
Trevor / 5

RULE 4:   Girls can participate in boys' activities or play with boys'
toys under the following conditions:

- They are accompanied by same-sex peers who also want to join in the activity.
- They are given permission to play by the boys.
- They are asked to play by the boys and join the boys in the activity.
- They do not take up a place needed by a boy.

> **Do you ever play with toys that are mostly for boys?**
> Sometimes I play with boy things with my dad. I have a race track with cars.
> **Do you ever play with boy things at school?**
> Sometimes me and my friends play with the blocks. When the boys say we can.
> **What if you wanted to play blocks and the boys said "No?"**
> Then I'd tell the teacher or go play with another toy. *Dawn / 6*

> **Do you play football or baseball or games like that?**
> Sometimes girls can play football.
> **Do you like playing it?**
> Yeah, but the boys take the ball and won't give it to us.
> **What do you do then?**
> Usually the girls go on the climbers. Except if it's my ball, and then we keep playing. *Cathy / 6*

If these assumptions drawn from the children's discussions about rules are valid, it is important to examine them in light of both the differences in the way that boys and girls play and what causes these differences. Asking children to talk about their play as they understand it is one means of accessing children's knowledge about the rule-making process.

One difference that becomes apparent in talking with the children is the degree of control that girls and boys perceive themselves as holding in play situations. Boys seem to feel that they are in control of their play behaviours at all times, controlling their own actions when playing in neutral activities as well as during boys' activities. Furthermore, boys indicated that they can successfully leave off playing girls' activities at any time, and only seem to be externally controlled by the unified wishes of their peer group. Some boys also indicated that they have control over girls' entry into their play and are more likely to allow girls limited entry if playing girls' or neutral activities than if playing boys' activities.

Why do boys like Nintendo so much?
Because they get all the games so they don't let the girls play it.
What if the girls want to play?
Girls can only play when I want them to.
Who do you think makes the rules that say certain games are only for girls or only for boys?
I think the coaches do. The men. And the boys. Yes. Ourselves make the rules. *Jimmy / 5*

Is there anything in your classroom that is a 'girl thing' that the boys never play with or hardly ever play with?
Nah. There's just boys' stuff in our room. But we let the girls play with it.
You mean there are some things in your room that are mostly boys' stuff but the girls are allowed to play with them?
Yeah. We're nice to them and let them play.
What things are those?
Oh, trucks and hopscotch and everything in the room. It's all for boys but girls can play. *Jason / 6*

Girls, on the other hand, only seem to feel that they have control of their play when they are playing activities designated for girls. In neutral situations the boys may choose to assume control and in boys' activities the boys seem always to be in control.

Why do you think blocks are a boys' toy?
Just because the boys get there first. And then they won't let the girls play.
Do boys and girls play together?
No, mostly girls with girls and boys with boys. But sometimes they let us play with them.
What would you do if you wanted to play with the blocks and the boys were playing?
I'd just ask them and see what they said. *Meri / 6*

Have you ever wanted to do boys' games?
Uh-uh.

Do you think you ever will?
No.
Why not?
Because the boys wouldn't let me. They'd say "Go do what we
say." That's because boys think boys' games are just for boys
and girls shouldn't play them. Some days there's just no sense in
asking. *Dawn / 6*

It appears to be a very complicated arrangement that children
work out when playing together about who is in control, an arrangement that is dependent on toy selection, same-sex play versus cross-
sex play, size of groupings, setting, and whether or not an adult is
physically close enough to be an external, controlling factor.

Research by Carlsson-Paige & Levin (1990) suggests that the
assignment of control exhibited in children's play styles is enforced
by the distinct differences between the toys manufactured for boys
and for girls.

Boys' toys channel them into being strong, dominant and
competitive. They involve boys in life and death issues and
keep them active and busy trying to "save the world." Girls'
toys channel them into being passive, helpful and "pretty."
They foster play that trivializes emotions and leaves very little
of substance for girls to make use of in their dramatic play.
They lock play into a pastel world of sugar-coated plots and
compartmentalized, partial feelings. (p. 93)

If, in fact, boys' toys channel them toward dominant roles while
girls' toys encourage passivity and dependence, this may be one
factor in the differences in children's acceptance of control in their
play behaviours.

Another reason that boys tend to be more controlling in play
situations may be due to the fact that girls move into same-sex
friendships without major episodes of conflict, while boys learn to
"fight out dominance issues with one another" (Pitcher & Schultz,
1983, p. 31). "Boys thus develop skills for negotiating control that
females are not prompted to develop in interaction with age-mates.
Boys need to develop strategies for competition and probably learn
to value these strategies more than girls do" (p. 37). These differ-

ences may also account for the increased competition and physical aggression boys display in their play with toys, games, and sports activities.

Some Specific Play Behaviours

In order to look more closely at other gender differences in play styles, five areas related to boys' and girls' activities will be examined in detail: doll play, sports, aggressive play, dancing, and dressing up. Because of the involved discussions raised repeatedly by the children in their responses, each of these areas will be discussed in detail.

Doll Play

There was little doubt amongst any of the children that dolls are a toy strongly associated with girls. In fact, certain dolls, such as Barbie dolls or baby dolls were identified as being exclusively for girls; boys were only allowed to play with boy dolls or stuffed animals resembling dolls, and even then, these were more acceptable as bedtime toys.

Can you think of any other things that you'd say were girl things?
Barbies. Dolls.
Are there any dolls that boys could play with?
Boy dolls.
Is it okay for boys to play with Ken dolls?
If they want to. But I don't think many want to.
If boys play with boy dolls would you still call dolls 'girl things'?
Yes, because dolls are mostly for girls and if boys play with them then they're playing with girl things.   *Dawn / 6*

Do you like dolls?
Not very much but my sister does. And I like stuffed animals.
Why don't you like dolls?
Because sometimes people laugh at me for liking dolls.
Do they laugh at your sisters for liking dolls?
No. They're girls and it's okay for them to like dolls. Other

people don't laugh at them like they laugh at me. It's okay for little boys to like dolls but not big boys. Then they laugh. *John / 6*

Carlsson-Paige & Levin suggest that dolls have become inextricably linked to girls by their association with 'feminine' clothing, make-up, and hairstyles; their sexually-defined body types, and their portrayal of accepted female behaviours. They cite consumer research which suggests that the manufacturing trend towards 'teenage' dolls—immersed in the adolescent world of men, dating, and glamorous parties—has replaced traditional baby dolls, which encourage children to act out family roles based on their own experiences.[5] Those baby dolls which are still available in stores must 'do something' in order to appeal to the children: gone are the soft, cuddly dolls who opened and closed their eyes, and in their place are those like P.J. Sparkles whose jewellery lights up when you press her tummy, Baby Oh-Oh who crawls to her own potty, and Magic Nursery Baby who is revealed as either a girl or a boy when a magic card is immersed in water.

Perhaps because even baby dolls are becoming more 'feminized', fewer parents are choosing to give dolls to young boys, and children are assuming at earlier ages that dolls are a girls' toy. Four-year-old David brought up the issue of dolls several times, trying to justify why he did not own one.

Do you ever play with dolls?
Yeah. My nana made my sister a doll.
Did she make you one, too?
No. Boys don't have dolls.
Why not?
I don't know. I like dolls. I play with my sister's dolls.
Do you have any stuffed toys that are sorta like dolls?
Yeah. I have a baseball doll. But I don't play with it really much.
Why not?
Because it's on my shelf. It's the kind of doll that you don't play with much. It might break. *David / 4*

The following day, David secretly whispered to me that he had bought a doll at a garage sale, justifying his purchase by saying that he planned to pretend it belonged to his sister.

Several other younger boys wistfully admitted their desire to play with dolls, but quickly followed up with a reminder that dolls were really a "girl toy." Some admitted to playing with their sisters' dolls or in a different setting, such as the classroom house-centre. It seems that 'private' doll play (i.e., within the safety of the home) or play suggested by an adult (i.e., a teacher) is perceived by children as being more acceptable for boys than doll play within a public setting.

In spite of this, several boys, including Brent and Jimmy, although curious about dolls, remained adamant that dolls were strictly a toy for girls.

> **What about playing with dolls?**
> (*chants*) It's for girls, girls, girls.
> **Is it okay for boys to play with dolls?**
> Some boys like dolls. But only baby boys like dolls.
> **So when boys get bigger they don't like dolls any more?**
> I sorta like dolls but I don't really like dolls.
> **Would you play with dolls at school?**
> (*chants*) Nope. Never, never, never. *Brent / 4*

> **What about playing with paper dolls?**
> (*shouting*) Girls! That's what girls do! That's what they're made for is girls! *Jimmy / 5*

Although many of the older boys responded emphatically that they no longer played with dolls, they implied that it might be acceptable for younger boys to play with dolls, as illustrated in these excerpts.

> **Do you think that the older you get the more boy things you like to do?**
> Yeah, I guess. When you get bigger you can't do girls' things.
> **Who says?**
> Everybody. They'd laugh. Boys do boys' things and girls do girls' things when you get in Grade One.
> **What about your little brother, does he like dolls?**
> Yes.

What about your big brother?
No. He's too old for dolls. *Paul / 5*

Do you ever play with dolls now that you're in Grade One?
Nope. Dolls are for girls and little kids.
Did you use to play with them?
No. The only doll I've ever got is a bedtime toy.
Is it okay for boys to take dolls to bed with them?
Yeah. *Matt / 6*

Other children commented that boys and girls played with dolls differently; whereas girls cared for them as if they were real babies, boys threw them around, used them for fighting, kidnapped them, saved them from fires, and took off their heads.

Yeah, me and my brother play with dolls. We take their heads off and then we torture them. It's really fun. *Jason / 6*

These findings are confirmed by Paley's research (1984) which traces the play styles of preschool boys in the house-centre as they grow older.

Domestic play looks remarkably alike for both sexes at age three....Mother, father and baby are the primary actors, but identities shift and the participants seldom keep one another informed....By the age of four, the boys are beginning to rebel. The girls prefer one mother, one father, and one baby per household...but some boys would rather be monsters or super-heroes. The four year-old boy seems less comfortable in the doll corner than he was the year before. By five, [the boys] have had enough doll-corner play. The more cohesive the boys' group, the more disruptive is its doll-corner play. As the superhero dominates boys' fantasy play the girls turn to dramatic plots that eliminate boys and bring in more sisters and princesses....Both seek a new social definition for 'boy' and 'girl'. (pp. x, xi)

My suggestion that superhero figures such as Ninja Turtles or Batman could be considered as appropriate dolls for boys was met by some opposition. When asked to clarify his reasoning, Matt replied:

> They'd be different. They're figures. Figures are for boys.
> Besides, boys play with them differently. They have weapons
> and you have to make funny sounds and fight. *Matt / 6*

It appears that the main objection to classifying superhero figures
as dolls revolves around children's assignment of certain toys to a
specific gender role. There seems to be a distinct need amongst the
boys to locate superhero figures—along with the power, strength,
and violence that they symbolize—within the male domain. Superhero figures offer boys acceptable alternatives to dolls. Carlsson-
Paige & Levin maintain that if classified as dolls, they would then
be recognized as girls' toys and therefore unavailable to boys.[6]

The impression given over and over again throughout the
children's discussions is that dolls are and should be a toy for girls.
This was clearly noted in Brent's response.

> Yes, I think all girls like dolls. But boys don't. And that's just
> the way it should be. Because they're girls' things you see. The
> police say so. If girls doesn't play with girls' things her would
> just go to jail. *Brent / 4*

After stopping to think for a moment, he added,

> Dolls are for girls. I'm a boy. It's okay for boys to like dolls if
> they want but they still shouldn't play with them.

His answer sums up the beliefs of the majority of the boys in the
study.

Sports

Whereas the children tended to locate doll play within the girls'
domain, sports were identified as an area owned almost exclusively
by boys. The general feeling seemed to be that boys control the
degree to which girls can be involved in sports by 'allowing' girls
to participate. This view was openly stated by many boys in the
study and tolerated, if not accepted, by most girls.

> **What are some things that you think boys are supposed to do?**
> We're allowed to play football and baseball. Girls aren't.

Do you think that it's a good idea for boys to learn baseball and football?
Yes.
More important than learning dancing and skipping?
Yes. Sports are better for boys. So that's just what boys should do. *Travis / 6*

Would you like it if girls could play baseball and basketball and those games without being teased?
Yeah, we have a net at home and I play basketball with my brother.
Are you as good as the boys are?
Yeah.
Are you better?
Sort of. Better than some boys.
Would boys say you're better?
Not likely. They'd say I'm a girl. My friend Tommy says it's not too likely that girls will ever be better than boys at sports. Even if they work really hard. *Cathy / 6*

When considering the current dominance of males in sport, it is not surprising that young boys want to control girls' entry into what is presently viewed as a male stronghold.[7] Since the physical evidence provided by the media, public leagues, and choice of activities on the playground supports boys' understanding that girls are less involved in this area, children seem to believe that it is the boys who control girls' participation.

Since the entry requirements for organized sport are not directly visible to young children, it is the physical skills required by the sport—strength, aggression, and toughness—which seem to have the strongest influence on children's perceptions of whether or not both girls and boys are allowed to play. Research by Bredemeier *et al.* confirms children's reliance on physical attributes, suggesting that the differing preferences of boys and girls are based on children's perceptions of the degree of contact required by the activity. They found that children associated such high-contact sports as karate and football strictly with boys, whereas low-contact sports such as swimming, gymnastics, and track were perceived as appropriate for both sexes. Significantly fewer girls than boys participated in sports such as baseball or soccer. These differences are attributed to the fact that "higher contact sports are more congruent with the traditional male gender role [and] girls are given little opportunity or encouragement to participate in them."[8]

These findings were reflected in the children's responses in this study, which showed that both boys and girls believe that boys are faster, stronger, braver, and tougher because they "have bigger muscles." The children considered football, hockey, soccer, and baseball—sports all requiring physical size, strength, and speed—to be within the boys' domain. It is worth noting that all of these sports are played professionally by adult males in televised games. Generally the children reported that basketball, swimming, and gymnastics were sports accessible to both sexes, and that girls would be allowed minimal entry into the modified form of T-ball, running activities, and skating.

> **Was it okay that Oliver wasn't good at baseball and football?**
> No, all boys should be good at those games. And hockey and wrestling, too.
> **Why is that?**
> Because they're boys.
> **Can girls be good at those games?**
> No. Girls don't really do sports. (*thinks*) Except maybe for swimming. And I do gymnastics and it's for girls. *Julie / 5*
>
> **What kinds of sports are boys good at?**
> Oh, I guess football and baseball and basketball.
> **Any others?**
> Well...let's see. Boys are good at hockey because they can skate. You know...all the strong sports.
> **What sports are girls good at?**
> Not many. They like dancing. Some girls play baseball but they don't hit as good.
> **Are there any sports that both boys and girls are good at?**
> Maybe swimming. And skating, too, but we're still faster.
> *Jason / 6*

Even though the boys agreed that girls could participate in some sports, it should be noted that this limited access was grudgingly given; many boys were quick to point out that, in sports, girls should never expect to be as good as their male counterparts, who are more competitive.

What other games are mostly for boys?
Football.
Could girls be good football players?
Nope. Not strong enough.
Any other games?
Baseball and soccer. You have to be fast to do that. You see, girls' problem is that they just can't run as good. *Jimmy / 5*

Why do you think boys like hockey so much?
They like it because they're good at winning.
Would girls like to play hockey, too?
Yeah, they can play, too. But they don't want to win so much.
Brent / 4

Girls' participation in this area seems to make many boys feel uneasy. Some boys solved this problem by insisting on separate teams. John reiterated over and over again why it would be best for everyone if girls and boys played separately.

What about football and baseball and basketball?
There's boys' football, boys' basketball, boys' baseball. But any of them can be for girls or boys if they have their own team.
Can boys and girls play on the same team?
No, 'cause they're different games when boys and girls play them. Different. The girls have to play on this space and the boys on this space. They're separate. There's different teams for that reason.
So boys and girls shouldn't ever play the games together?
Nope. Never. That's just how it should be. *John / 6*

Research into the success of co-educational sports indicates that more and more boys are agreeing with John, preferring to play sex-segregated sports. Monagan suggests that the move towards single-sex sports is being led by males for several reasons. One justification, provided by coaches, is that both boys and girls under the age of 12 learn individual skills more quickly when playing with members of their own sex. A second reason given is that girls threaten the integrity of boys' sports, since boys place far greater emphasis on winning than do girls; as long as there are girls on the team, boys feel they will be unable to play with the same intensity and competitive drive as they would on an all-boy squad. The most startling information provided by Monagan, however, is that "most boys are scared to death of losing to girls and...subsequently facing a loss of self-esteem." He quotes Rainer Martens, coach of the United States Olympic team: "Given today's norms in our society, when competing with girls, many boys experience considerable psychological stress because they feel that losing to a female will bring shame."[9]

Most of the girls in the study felt they could successfully play the sports they wished to play, although they seemed to recognize that many boys do not welcome their participation in this area.

> **So is hockey a girls' game or a boys' game or both?**
> It could be both. More boys play it though.
> **Why is that?**
> They think it's just for boys and that girls shouldn't play it.
> *Leann / 5*

Although recognizing it, none of the girls questioned the fairness or rightness of their exclusion from certain sports, seemingly accepting it as a natural occurrence. Most barely seemed interested. However, upon considering the dearth of female media and parental role models available for young girls, along with the fact that most sports are organized and coached by males, it should not be surprising that sports is an area which girls prefer to leave for boys.

Furthermore, upon talking with them, it appears that girls have justified in their own minds that their lack of participation in sports is self-chosen. Even at four years of age, girls seem to have learned to view sports as an area which requires intense activity, physical roughhousing, and a strong competitive drive, aspects which either do not interest them or which they consider socially unacceptable for females. It seems as if there are more important things in young girls' lives, and organized sports can be put off until they decide whether or not they wish to become involved.

Can you think of any boy things?
Playing football 'cause girls don't usually play that.
Why do you think girls don't play football?
'Cause they don't usually like to run that much and be tackled to the ground and jumped on.
Do boys like that part?
I don't think so but they keep on doing it, so maybe.   *Meri / 6*

Well, how about you? Do you do any boy things?
Well I will do karate. And I did do baseball once but I wasn't very good at it and I didn't like it.
If you practised at baseball, do you think you would be as good as the boys or even better?
Maybe better.
So do you think if girls practise hard they can be as good or even better than boys at sports?
Yeah, but only if they want to practise. Some girls don't want to do those things. Like I don't like baseball very much.
Dawn / 6

Thus, the role which most girls willingly assume with regard to sports seems to be a passive one; they enjoy maintaining the potential of being able to participate but seem to discard the actual desire to become actively involved. Although boys may feel that males hold the decision-making rights within this area, including control over girls' entry into sport, the girls appear to counter this attempt at control by rationalizing that they do not wish to participate.

Aggressive Play
Part of the reason that children classify sports within the male domain is based on their belief that boys are more aggressive and can therefore handle the roughness required by high-contact, competitive sports. It seems as if aggression has become a male-associated trait, one which boys feel is required of them. In a study by Hyde (1984b) boys described themselves as more physically aggressive than girls in both sports and daily-life contacts. Such a belief is made evident over and over again in this study through boys' choice of toys and their elected style of play. Throughout our discussions of toy choices, boys regularly listed superhero action

figures (Wrestlers, Ninja Turtles, Batman, and Superman), war toys
(GI Joes, army tanks, and guns), and Nintendo games involving
fighting, shooting, and spying as their favourite toys. The form of
play these toys promoted was described by both boys and girls as
active, aggressive, and often violent.[11]

Do you think GI Joes are good toys for boys and girls?
Yeah. For boys. Because they can do kicks and beat up the cobra.
Usually GI Joes win every day.
Do they have weapons?
Yeah…laser guns, machine guns, grenades, and they shoot peo-
ple. *Jason / 6*

What kinds of games do you like to play?
A Nintendo game…Saiga. At the end there's this big huge thing
that throws bullets and bombs at you and blows you up. And
there's a guy at the top shooting at you and you have to blow these
things up.
What else do you like to do?
Play with the tough animals and make them beat each other up.
I play GI Joes on the climbers and pretend that I have toy knives
and toy guns. Sometimes I play army.
How do you play army?
Easy. All you have to do is get a pretend gun and keep on shooting
pretend people.
Could girls play that, too?
Just boys. Girls don't like fighting. *Jimmy / 5*

The pretend actions of the toys that boys play with are often
carried over into their preferred style of play with each other; boys
in the study described themselves practising a form of "play fighting" including such behaviours as throwing each other to the
ground, roughhousing, wrestling, karate kicking, and chasing. Although no girls described themselves as playing in this manner, the
girls seemed aware of this form of play carried out by boys, most
often electing to give it a wide berth.

Is there anything boys do better than girls?
Beating up but I can't get beat up by them 'cause I either run away
or say I don't want to play.

Do you ever think of fighting a boy back?
No, 'cause I'll get hurt I think, so I don't go to them.
What do you think about fighting?
It's not okay for girls to fight.
Is it okay for boys to fight?
Yes, but not girls. That's the rule.   *Ann / 4*

The end result of this style of play is that aggressive behaviour and physical violence become associated with boys, who then expect this type of behaviour of the male characters that they encounter in stories.

In three of the stories, the male characters—Jesse, Oliver, and Ronald—do not act the way that boys expect them to act. Therefore, many of the boys agreed that it was appropriate for Oliver and Jesse to be labelled "sissies" and even stated that they would call them names in similar circumstances. Davies refers to this adherence to their understanding of how boys should act as "reciprocity" or "the active reflecting back to the other of the other's self."[12] In this case, the boys feel that it is more acceptable to label Oliver Button and Jesse as "sissies" and continue to believe that's what they are, than for boys to extend or modify their own conception of appropriate play behaviours for males.

The children's reactions to Ronald's character were also negative, providing further insight into how they believe boys should act. They commented over and over again on his cowardice at being unwilling to attempt an escape from the dragon's cave, behaviour they thought to be inappropriate for a male. They were all far braver and wiser than he, and would take on the dragon without hesitation.

If you were Ronald and were stuck in that room, what would you do?
I'd just escape...by breaking the bar, climbing out, going on the lock, jumping on the dragon's head and running away.
So you wouldn't be frightened of that dragon?
Nope. I'm brave. That guy's a wimp 'cause he just sits there.
John / 6

Ronald was also viewed negatively for not attempting to get away from the dragon as he was carried off. Most of the children had

solutions for how they would escape in his place.   The girls'
responses generally focussed on ways to avoid getting caught or
upon non-violent means of escape.[13]

> **What would you do if one day you woke up and a dragon was
> trying to kidnap you?**
> I don't know. I'd probably hide in my sleeping bag.
> *Mandy / 4*
>
> I'd just trick him. I'd climb up high and then he wouldn't get me.
> *Ann / 4*

Cathy is an interesting exception, combining violent and non-violent
means:

> First I'd tickle him until he dropped me. And then I'd pull his
> tail off.   *Cathy / 6*

In contrast, the boys' actions overall were more aggressive, often
relying on physical violence to solve the problem.

> **What would you do if a dragon tried to kidnap you?**
> I would get a hose and blow the fire right out of his mouth.
> *Bryan / 4*
>
> Well, I wouldn't let him catch me, but if he did I'd just kick him
> in the nuts.   *Travis / 6*
>
> I would just have to get a sword and chop his head off.
> *Jimmy / 5*

The children in the study also had a tendency to link aggression
with the physical characteristics that they identified as 'male'. The
character Ronald was not well-liked by any of the children, leaving
the 'male' dragon as the only male character with which the boys
could identify. In addition to physical characteristics, the children
labelled the dragon by using the male-associated, aggressive characteristics he displayed—namely, toughness, meanness, strength,
bravery, speed, and the ability to breathe fire.

Is there anything that dragon did that makes you think it's a boy dragon?
He was tough. He could carry this boy. So he was tough and strong.
Do you think Elizabeth was tough?
Yeah. But she's a girl. Most boys are tough.
Why is that?
Because they're boys. Boys are supposed to be tougher than girls. Girls can just be a little tough and they don't usually show it.
Leann / 5

I think it must be a boy because sometimes boys get more tired than girls because they work harder than girls.
Anything else?
Well, boys waste all their air because they run a lot. *Meri / 6*

In sum, the children's responses reveal that both boys and girls perceive and accept aggression as a common occurrence in boys' preferred style of play. Girls are more likely to act as observers, avoiding aggressive play, a solution which the boys interpret as best "because they're girls."

Dancing

The area of dance is one that is disturbing for both girls and boys. It is problematic for girls because, at a very young age, they learn that dancing is something that mostly girls do, and are therefore pressured towards accepting it as feminine. However, this area is also problematic for boys, who realize that although dance as an art form is dominated by girls and women, it is also an expected leisure activity in the development of heterosexual relationships. During adolescence, for example, not only are boys expected to participate in dancing as part of a mating ritual, but they are expected, according to McRobbie,[15] to show mastery and domination of male-female dancing. Faced with such apparent contradictions, it is not surprising that amongst both girls and boys, Oliver's success at tap dancing caused consternation.

When asked to state whether dancing is something done by girls or boys, most children readily categorized dancing as a 'girl thing'.

Even David, one of the few boys who admitted that he liked to dance, particularly as he owned a red skirt that he would put on at home and twirl around and around, was quick to note that he could never take dancing lessons because he was not a girl. The youngest children in the study justified their reasoning with reference to visible cues: in order to dance, you have to wear a dress; only girls wear dresses, therefore only girls should be dancers. Others talked about the fact that dancers must look pretty or have long hair or perform movements commonly demonstrated by women.

Why do you think girls like dancing better than boys do?
Because they twirl around and they have dresses on.
Would it be alright for a boy to wear a dress to dancing school?
No, because that's not the thing that boys wear.
What if a boy danced in something else, like shorts?
That wouldn't be right. Girls wear dresses and are dancers.
Mandy / 4

What about dancing, who likes that best?
Girls.
Why do girls like dancing better than boys?
Because they look better at it. They can be pretty.
Does anything else make girls better at dancing?
Well, they practise more so they're better. And they have long hair and they twirl. That's what makes them good dancers.
Jill / 4

Who do you think goes to dancing school mostly, boys or girls or both?
Girls.
Why do you think mostly girls go?
Because they are girls. That's what girls do.
Is dancing a girl thing then?
Yes it is. They do the lessons. Girls have the right dresses. The boys don't.
Can you wear something else and go to dancing class?
Yeah. They can dance with nothing on. But you need dancing dresses to really dance. *David / 4*

From these descriptions, it appears that the picture many young children have of dancing is one of ballerinas, graceful movements, and beautiful costumes—all attributes associated with women.

These impressions held by the children are not surprising according to McRobbie's research, which examined the cultural and social influences dance has for both men and women. She suggests that dance has become closely linked with femininity through its reliance on costumes, body poses, facial expressions, and styles of movement commonly associated with women. However, the problem, as McRobbie sees it, lies in the knowledge that dance has also become a vehicle used to objectify and exploit the women who have achieved success at it by "positioning women as objects of the [male] gaze....Many of the movements and the conventions of dance have been so naturalized we hardly notice them, e.g., the inviting 'foxy' expressions on the dancers' faces, the up-the-thigh shot, followed by the smiling complicit wink to the camera."[16]

I stated earlier that associating dancing with a specific gender seems to create conflict for the children in another way, particularly for the boys when they realize that boy-girl dancing is an accepted leisure activity. Up until adolescence, dancing is inextricably linked with femininity; however, during the teenage years it becomes a valued part of the heterosexual courtship routine. Suddenly, it is not only acceptable but desirable for boys to participate in what they have always considered to be a feminine behaviour.

Hence it is worth noting the varying ways the children in this study handled the conflict presented by boy-girl dancing. Many of the youngest children, both girls and boys, tended to rely most heavily on their known beliefs by either ignoring the conflicting information which was being introduced in the story or weighing it against what they already believed to be true.

Is dancing something that's mostly for girls or mostly for boys or both?
For both...sometimes boys and girls dance together. Well, but it's really for girls. Because girls are supposed to wear skirts, not boys.
So who do you think dancing is for?
Well considering what they wear for dancing I guess it's for girls.

> Girls are supposed to play girls' things and boys are supposed to do boys' things so it must be just for girls.   *Jill / 4*

Jill realizes that both boys and girls participate in dancing; however, her visual picture of dancers as female overrides her developing background knowledge.

Meri and Leann, being older and having additional knowledge with which to contend, accept dancing as 'a girl thing' but allocate boys some control over the activity. Their willingness to relinquish control allows the boys to participate in boy-girl dancing without threat to their masculinity.

> **Why do you think girls are the best dancers?**
> I think that girls joined up first because girls like dancing the most.
> **Why is it that girls like to dance so much?**
> Because it's a girl thing.
> **Who tells them it's a girl thing?**
> Boys. They decide what are girl things and what are boy things and they tell us.   *Meri / 6*
>
> **Why do you think girls like dancing better?**
> 'Cause they can dance with the boys. That's why they go…to learn.
> **What about the boys learning how to dance with the girls?**
> They don't need to learn how. They just can do it. Or else maybe boys go to boy dancing class.   *Leann / 5*

These two excerpts show the line of reasoning that young children often adopt in explaining their understanding of gendered behaviours. Girls like dancing and are good at it; therefore dancing must be a 'girl thing'.

However, in order to justify boys' participation in what has thus far been considered 'a girl thing', many girls return the control of the activity to the boys. McRobbie suggests that by doing so, girls and women are resigning themselves once again to accepting the less powerful 'feminine' role within the male-female relationship.[17] Perhaps young girls do perceive couple dancing as an activity that is controlled by males since, in most cases, it is the boys who choose the girls as partners; however, I am not certain that children are sophisticated enough to evaluate partner dancing in terms of its sexual intent. It may simply be that girls understand and accept boys' hesitation to enter into a 'feminine' activity, and encourage their participation by giving them control. Regardless of their reasoning, it is important to note that, in the present study, the girls seemed less willing to take on responsibility for their own actions in girl-boy activities.

The older boys in the study justified their entrance into a feminine activity in yet another way, by seeking cultural acceptability for boys' dancing. Paul and John justify their positions by suggesting that boys dance differently than girls.

> **Do you think dancing is a boy thing or a girl thing or for both?**
> A girl thing.
> **Why do girls like dancing?**
> Because boys usually dance boys' stuff and girls dance girls' stuff.
> **Do you mean that boys can do dancing but they do it differently than girls?**
> Well, girls dance in a row for dancing class. Boys can do the same thing but boys usually dance different because dancing is usually for girls so they want to dance different. *Paul / 5*

> **Do you think dancing is something for girls or boys or both?**
> Both. If it's soft music it's for girls and if it's rock and roll it's for boys.
> **But can girls do rock and roll?**
> They don't know very much about music. You see, dancing is part of acting. It's just that boys can dance if it's rock and roll and girls can dance if it's soft music. Maybe Oliver was doing rock and roll dancing so that's okay. *John / 6*

The justification by these two boys is not so very different from that stated by McRobbie (1986) in her explanation of how men are now able to enter the feminine world of dancing.

> Men can now demonstrate sophisticated dancing styles with expertise and pleasure without inviting criticism or disdain amongst their male peers. Black (Afro-Caribbean) culture has done much to bring about the change with the massive increase in dance technology ('ghetto-blasters' and walkmen, hi'fi's and

> sound systems, 12" singles and pop videos) and in dance music
> style (funk, rap, disco, soul, lovers rock, and pop) advertising
> its appeal and facilitating its spread. Most new dance styles
> have come out of black youth culture with men tending to take
> up the most spectacular gymnastic and acrobatic variations.
> (p. 144)

It appears as if, in order to make the feminine world of dance more
acceptable, men and boys are searching for ways to make it more
masculine. The evolution of dance over time will provide the
evidence of their success or failure.

Dressing Up

Playing dress up, and the fantasy play that accompanies this
behaviour, was the final area that children viewed as being different
for girls and for boys. Discussions about this play behaviour arose
in response to two books—*Oliver Button Is a Sissy* (dressing up was
one of the activities Oliver enjoyed playing) and *Jesse's Dream Skirt*
(Jesse's classmates discussed dressing up in opposite-sex clothing).
'Playing dress up' was defined by the children as putting on clothing
or a costume and pretending to be someone or something else,
generally acting out the role that the clothing suggests. The children
separated this form of play from Jesse's behaviour since he was no
longer *pretending* when he chose to wear a skirt to school.

When initially asked about dressing up, most children classified
it as an activity which mainly girls play; however, upon further discussion, the children agreed that boys could play dress up provided
they only wore male-associated clothing and assumed male roles.
Although girls were expected to wear female-associated clothing
and assume female roles, if a male character was needed and no
boys were willing to play, it was acceptable for girls to dress up in
boys' clothing and take on a male role.

Do you ever dress up?
Yeah. But only in boys' dress-up clothes.
What clothes do you wear?
Any boys' dress-up clothes. Like pants. Or a shirt. A boy's
shirt not a girl's shirt. Or a boy's bathing suit. Or a hat.
Are there any clothes that just boys can wear and not girls?

I already told you. Just boys' dress-up clothes. Girls have their own clothes like skirts and stuff.
Do girls ever wear boys' clothes?
Only if they want to be a daddy. And they shouldn't do that. Only boys should. *John / 6*

Who do you think can play dress up?
Well, boys can play but they never do. They're getting too old for that. So, just the girls I guess.
Do you think it's okay for girls and boys to dress up in their dad's old clothes and pretend they're daddies?
Yeah, it's okay for boys but I'm not sure about girls.
Why not?
Well, I guess it's okay if they can't find a boy.
Could boys dress up and pretend to be mommy?
Well they never do. Boys just aren't like that.
Why don't boys dress up in girls' clothes?
Because they're boys and their friends would laugh. *Leann / 5*

Although several children admitted to dressing up in opposite-sex clothing at home, most felt that this behaviour was inappropriate for the public world of school. Children who ignored these rules and dressed up in opposite-sex clothing often did so deliberately to get a laugh from classmates. Paul compared this behaviour to that of a wrestling star who wears skirts.

Why do you think (the wrestler) wears a skirt?
I don't know. Maybe to look funny 'cause it makes him look like a girl. Then he twirls around and around and everyone laughs and laughs. But he always fights so the audience knows he's strong, not like a girl. I guess he likes that because he's just pretending. I don't think he'd do it for real. *Paul / 5*

One of the fears that the children voiced regularly was being mistaken for a member of the opposite sex, a concern that seemed more worrisome for the boys.

Would you ever dress up like that in your mom's or your dad's clothes?
Just my dad's.

Why not your mom's?
My brothers would think I look funny.
Would you ever try on a skirt or a dress from the dress-up box at school?
No way! My teacher would think I was a girl.
Couldn't you just say, "I'm really a boy. I'm just pretending to be a girl?"
Nope. I don't even want to look like a girl. My friends would laugh.   *Trevor / 5*

Do you think Dawn looks like a boy because she's wearing that baseball uniform?
No.
Why not?
She just looks like a girl.
Would it matter if someone thought she was a boy?
No. She could just tell them. That's all she needs to do.
Kendra / 5

Would it be a problem if people thought the boys were girls?
Not for little boys. My next door neighbour is a little boy and he wears some dresses when his sister wears dresses. It's not a problem. He just says he's not a girl.
What about bigger boys?
They should just say, "I'm not a girl. I'm a boy, too." But they don't like to do that because people still think they'll act like girls.
Mandy / 4

It seems that if a girl is assumed to be a boy, she can just say, "I'm a girl" and the incident will be forgotten, whereas a boy suffers additional social consequences such as teasing or ridicule.

The boys' fears were reinforced in the literature presented to the children; Oliver is teased and called names by the boys in his class and Mike's father yells at him for dressing up in his mother's clothing. Most of the boys agreed that Mike and Oliver were wrong to dress up, whereas the girls were more accepting of these behaviours.

Was that a good idea for Mike to dress up in his mother's clothes?

No. Because he's a boy.
But is it okay if he just pretends to be a girl?
No. That would be wrong. Maybe he could dress up in his dad's clothes but not his mother's.
Would you ever dress up in your mother's clothes?
My dad would say, "No way." I don't even dress up in my dad's clothes. *Trevor / 6*

Was it okay for Oliver to dress up in that hat and scarf and dance around?
Yeah. That was okay. His dad shouldn't have got mad at him.
Why do you think his father was upset?
Because he's a boy and those are girl clothes.
Is that okay for him to dress up in girl clothes?
Yeah. As long as he doesn't do it all the time. *Mandy / 4*

Davies suggests that the differences in boys' and girls' willingness to dress in opposite-sex clothing are because girls are less sex-typed than boys in their conception of what is acceptable for their gender role, and thus enjoy the advantage of a wider range of behaviours. As a result, girls are able to act out masculine roles without fear that they will lose their feminine identity. Boys, however, operate under the social belief that part of acting masculine consists of not acting like a girl. Thus, boys interpret maleness as not only continually portraying behaviours which are masculine, but also the avoidance of feminine behaviours.[18]

Associating certain female traits with boys is not encouraged, accounting for the number of negative proscriptions with which boys are socialized. Boys are repeatedly warned by parents, peers, teachers, storybook characters, and the media not to act like a sissy, not to cry, not to play with dolls, along with the ultimate insult—not to act like a girl. Instead, they are reinforced with specifically male-defined comments such as "Be a little man" or "You're the man of the family now." The underlying implication is that the male role, though more restrictive, is strong, powerful, and dependable, while the female role, though more flexible and less restrictive, is nonetheless weaker, emotional, and dependent.

It is not surprising, then, that when dressing up, the costumes that children select and the roles that they act out are influenced by their attempts to reinforce a specific gender identity as either a girl or a boy. Pitcher & Schultz (1983) conclude that:

> Boys play more varied and global roles that are more characterized by fantasy and power. Boys' sex roles tend to be functional, defined by action plans. Characters are usually stereotyped and flat with habitual attitudes and personality features (cowboy, foreman, Batman, Superman). Girls prefer family roles, especially the more traditional roles of daughter and mother. Even at the youngest age, girls are quite knowledgeable about the details and subtleties in these roles. (p. 79)

In this study, the children's need to identify themselves with the traditional male-female roles was readily apparent when they were asked how they would dress up if provided with pieces of material. Pretending to be princesses, mothers and fine ladies, the girls would make dresses, skirts, and veils in order to dance, care for babies, and serve tea. Pretending to be pirates, superheroes, and Ninja Turtles, the boys would make capes, headbands, and sashes in order to fight with weapons and save the world.

Their ongoing adherence to these traditional roles, if somewhat disconcerting when one recognizes the limitations of the choices for both sexes, may be representational of the world children have experienced thus far. The world which these young children described would seem to be the familiar one of the conventional. Through the eyes of children, fathers represent powerful family leaders and money-makers who do not need to involve themselves with child care tasks; it is a mother's job to have the babies, care for growing children, cook the meals, and clean the house, even if she is working outside the home.[19]

What's a mom's job?
To have a baby and feed it and change it and walk it. Girls do that.
Anything else?
Yeah. She has to wash clothes and cook.
Even if she has a job outside the house to go to each day?

Yup. That's what moms are supposed to do. Housework.
What's a dad's job?
Nothing. He doesn't have to do anything at home. His job is to
watch TV. *Jimmy / 5*

Whose job do you think it is to look after a baby?
A mom's. Not a dad's.
What should a dad do?
He has to go out and work and make money from the bank to buy
the food. But the mom cooks it. *Jill / 4*

Is it dad's job to change a baby's diapers?
No. Moms do that. Dads go out and do things. They have to
work for a living instead. *Jason / 6*

Having looked at the role of visible markers and play behaviours
in young children's evolving conceptions about gender, we turn
now to the equally powerful influence of social relationships and
rules.

4 / Social Relationships and Rules

Social Relationships

When the children were asked to state whom they played with the most, their responses indicated that boys preferred to play with boys, while girls preferred to play with girls. Even though several children responded that they played with both boys and girls, the list of friends they gave seldom included more than one child of the opposite sex, often a sibling.

Tell me about your friends.
I like to play more with boys than with girls. I don't play with girls much.
Why do you like playing with boys more?
Because they like to play with me and do the things I like to do. They like to play baseball and that's a game that's mostly for boys. *Barry / 4*

Who do you like playing with the best?
I really like playing with just girls.
Why is that?
I've always played with girls. I like them better.
Would you ever like to play with boys?
No. They make me play their games and I don't like playing boys' games. *Ann / 4*

Are most of your friends girls or boys or both?
Mostly girls. But I play with a few boys sometimes. My brother's friends.
Why do you think most of your friends are girls?
I don't know. They just are. They're the same as me so they like

the same things. I just don't like boys much I guess, or their yucky toys either. *Leann / 5*

The reason given by most children was clear; same-sex friends like to do the same things, generally activities restricted to one sex or the other. The children also suggested that, although same-sex friends were preferable, mixed-sex groupings were allowed, provided boys did not just play with girls or girls just play with boys.

In examining same-sex relations, Pitcher & Schultz supported the children's conceptions of peer choices, citing that by age three, girls form same-sex alliances through positive interactions whereas same-sex encounters amongst boys generally do not occur until age four. "By age 4, boys are no longer paying as much attention to girls, but are paying much more attention to one another. In other words, boy/boy relations are forming at the expense of boy/girl relations."[1] They attribute the differences to two factors; first, that girls mature earlier than boys, resulting in fewer aggressive incidents and better social relations, and second, that boys have a greater initial difficulty determining their gender identity since their early years are spent in an environment which is created and maintained by females. Because children of both sexes initially identify with the parent responsible for child care, and because this figure is most often female, both at home and at school, it follows that boys will have more difficulty relating to same-sex peers.

A preference for same-sex play at this age can be justified by other reasons already cited within this study. First, it has been noted that children categorize favourite toys as being suitable for either girls or boys. Therefore, in order to be involved in mixed-sex play, the children would have to agree on acceptable 'neutral' toys, thus eliminating their own favourites—dolls, vehicles, superhero figures, and sports equipment. As well, girls and boys play differently (as we have seen in Chapter 3)—boys' play being aggressive, dominant, and competitive and girls' play being passive, quiet, and more domesticated, it is not surprising that children would note these differences. Pitcher & Schultz refer to this period of competition for control as "vying for power," during which boys fight out dominance issues with one another. Because of the need to dominate, male friendships form differently than female friendships, with boys' play showing a high degree of conflict as they relate to one another, while girls relate more positively.[2] Thus, because of varying toy preferences and play styles, it seems less likely that boys and girls would want to play together.

Another issue raised earlier in this study, suggesting that boys control girls' entry into their play space and that girls allow their entry to be sanctified by boys, may also help explain why mixed-sex play is less common. In any play relationship, certain children are more dominant over others. In girl-boy play, however, evidence from this study indicates that the boys expect to be the dominant ones, as shown by their use of such phrases as "Girls can only play when I want them to" or "We don't let the girls play it."[3]

The issue of control as it applies to mixed-sex play situations has been discussed previously; boys have been shown to exhibit control of mixed-sex play activities through aggressive actions, verbal management, and dominant behaviours.[4] If girls were willing to question their exclusion from certain play activities by boys, this might not present a problem; however, girls seem willing to allow boys to control girls' participation, withdrawing to their own activities and confined space. Perhaps girls already perceive boys as being more powerful because of the increased strength, speed, and size associated with adult males. Or perhaps girls choose to return to the activity at another time, thus avoiding the verbal or physical confrontations that often accompany their participation in mixed-sex play. The girls in this study seemed unable to explain why they did not want to play with boys, blaming girls' lack of participation on the boys' behaviours. Dawn commented, "The boys would say 'Go do what we say!'...so some days there's just no sense in asking them." Some researchers suggest that this withdrawal from play and ignoring of the boys may be the girls' attempt at control through a more subtle form of power strategy.[5] However, because boys measure power through dominant actions, they themselves do not view this behaviour as being powerful. In addition, because the boys' responses also showed that they feel entry into girls' play would label them as 'sissies', it becomes clearer why girls and boys play less frequently together.

Rules: The Assignment of Control

One of the questions I repeatedly asked the children throughout the study was: "Who makes the rules about the ways that boys and girls should behave?" Although girls occasionally claimed that boys made the rules, most children assigned the control of the decision making elsewhere, to people or institutions whom they felt traditionally had control over their actions—parents, teachers, principals, coaches, and police officers.

> **Who do you think makes the rules about how boys and girls should act or dress or what they should play with?**
> Well, I think that maybe the school principal decides what kids wear to school. And maybe moms and dads get to decide what kids play with. All I know is that kids don't make them.
> *Jason / 6*
>
> Maybe I think polices makes the rules. They're the bosses. Actually it's the boss of all the polices who makes the rules.
> *Brent / 4*
>
> The teachers I think. All the big people. They make all the rules that tell us what to do. Except for the rules that are really important and God makes those up and then He bosses them around. *Bryan / 4*
>
> Well it's not the girls that's for sure. Even boys try to tell us what to do. Like my brother. But I just don't listen to him.
> *Cathy / 6*

This view of adults as being more powerful than children is understandable, given children's experiences at home, at school, and through exposure to television. With the question of whether or not boys should be allowed to wear skirts, however, over a third of the children stated that this decision was controlled by God.

> **Who do you think makes that rule that boys shouldn't wear skirts to school?**
> It's probably God. Yeah, God. He probably makes that rule.

Is it okay to break that rule sometimes?
Yeah, it's okay but God won't like it.   *Meri / 6*

Would that be okay if the boys came to school looking like girls?
No, it wouldn't. Boys should look like boys.
Why is that so important?
Because...because...boys are made to look like boys and girls are made to look like girls. That's the rule, okay.
Who do you think makes that rule?
God. He's the one. The important one.
Do you think parents can help decide that rule?
No, 'cause God has a bigger brain than them...bigger even than me.   *John / 6*

In one sense, it is not surprising that children assigned this control omnipotently, since, regardless of religious training, many young children view God as being the ultimate controller of lives.[5] By being attributed to an unseen figure, not only is the decision strengthened, but it cannot conceivably be questioned, as can decisions made by parents or teachers. Perhaps from the children's perceptions, a boy choosing to wear a skirt is significant enough to require God's attention.

These impressions of external control by others suggest that power is beginning to become important in young children's lives; however, I remain unsure of how clearly children actually understand it. Power is certainly a difficult construct for children to grasp, since they judge it according to how it directly affects their own lives—for example, in the form of a bigger child who bullies them, a teacher who controls their behaviour, or a parent who protects them. Children lack the global view of power and the political notions that accompany an adult's perception of it. As a result, children measure power in terms of physical size, strength, and accompanying actions, although many of them seem to be beginning to associate intelligence with being powerful.

Based on a current societal structure which relegates women's power to a domestic sphere, particularly in relation to children, while legitimizing male power in every other social context,[6] there seems to be a need to examine children's understanding and utilization of power. Because of the male-female roles they see modelled daily at home, children may expect power to be demonstrably different for men and women, and subsequently reflect these differences in their play situations. Davies suggests that the degree of power a teacher holds over students also confirms children's understanding of power; in an authoritarian classroom where the teacher shares none of the control with the students, children come to accept power differentials between adults and children as a societal truth.[7]

It is not within the scope of this study to address how children perceive power or, indeed, if they differentiate between power held by boys and girls, or mothers and fathers. As a researcher, although confident that children demonstrate power within their play relations, I am unsure whether or not they understand the form of control they are using, or even if they are experienced enough with it to perceive their actions as powerful. The trends which I have introduced showing that boys act out superhero roles, practise karate, and talk about being stronger, faster, and smarter, while girls act out princesses and ladies-in-waiting, practise child care, and talk about clothing preferences, suggest that children's chosen behaviours at this age are already replicating the social patterns they see modelled. Children's conceptions of power, particularly in relation to their understanding of the power differentials in society, is certainly an area worthy of further study.

The Social Implications of Not Conforming: Conflict and Uncertainty

Based on their responses, it appears that these children regularly must decide between doing what they *want* to do and doing what they perceive they *should* do. The 'wants' are determined by their own desires, their personal likes and dislikes resulting from past experiences, and are influenced by input from parents, peers, and the media. The 'shoulds' are determined by the way children perceive that boys and girls are expected to act, based on 'moral lessons' from those who hold control over them—significant adults, their peer group, the media, the school, and God. The conflict in this area was evident over and over again as the children repeatedly contradicted themselves in their responses, trying to work out an understanding of gender in their own minds.

Do you ever play with dolls?
Yeah. My nana made my sister a doll.
Did she make you one, too?
No. Boys don't have dolls.
Why not?
I don't know. I like dolls.
Do you think it's fun for boys to do things that are mostly for girls, like dolls?
Maybe. No, boys shouldn't do girl things because they're boys.
Is it fun for you to play with your sister's doll?
Yeah. It's fun. For girls I mean. Not for boys. *David / 4*

What do you think about boys wearing a skirt to school?
Some kids would make fun of you.
Would you ever want to wear a skirt to school?
Yeah.
Would you do it one day?
No, because kids would make fun of you.
What if you knew they wouldn't make fun of you?
No. Maybe. Yeah, if no one made fun of me. But people would make fun so I won't wear one. *Travis / 6*

Who do you think is smarter, Elizabeth, Ronald, or the dragon?
Elizabeth, because she tricked the dragon.
Who do you think are smarter, girls or boys?
Boys, of course.
Then why wasn't Ronald smarter than Elizabeth?
He was smarter. Well no, he's just a stupid boy. But boys are still smarter than girls. *John / 6*

An examination of the children's responses to all four stories shows, overall, a great deal of variation. Sometimes, the children said one thing and then, either changed their minds or unknowingly refuted themselves; at other times, they gave different answers to the same question, asked in response to two different stories. This high degree of variation in their responses is supported by data which indicates that, at this age-level, children's beliefs about gendered behaviours are continually changing as they sort out new information, and may not yet be fully formed conceptually. As Davies (1988) puts it,

> What it means to be male or female in our society is complex and often contradictory. Each child develops a pattern of accommodation and resistance to the varied messages, approximating as closely as they can what they take to be correct "genderedness." (p. 10)

The difference in the children's responses may be partially attributed to their ages; very young children, less aware of the rules of behaviour accepted by society are more strongly governed by their desires and tend to respond by doing whatever they want. By about age three, however, children have learned many of the unwritten social rules which designate appropriate presentation of self as either male or female, and they begin to question whether or not they should participate in what are specifically labelled as non-conventional behaviours.[8]

Other differences may be the result of the varying experiences and beliefs that children encounter as they widen their social world. One boy in the study, who came from an acting family where both boys and girls were encouraged to sing and dance, had difficulty accepting his peer group's decision that dancing was only for girls. He overcame this conflict by modifying the rule—claiming that whereas girls dance to classical music, boys dance to rock and roll. Still other children created their own rules, making them fit their conceptions of the ways that boys and girls should behave.

Is it okay that Oliver keeps on dancing at the end?
Yeah, it's okay. He knows it's a girl thing. But he should learn to do boys' things too, like football and baseball.
Why is that?
Well, boys are allowed to do girl things provided they don't just do girl things. *Meri / 6*

Is it okay if girls play sports?
Only some sports. Like swimming. They shouldn't do football
or hockey unless their parents make them. *Jason / 6*

However, in changing or creating rules, children continue to rely
on society's willingness to accept the modified behaviour, knowing
that if they encounter resistance (i.e., in the form of peer ridicule),
they can quickly return to behaviours sanctified by their peer group
and surrounding adults.

The children also responded differently depending on whose
behaviour they were being asked to judge, their own behaviour or
that of the storybook character. When the children were asked whether or not Oliver should keep on dancing now that the boys liked
him, some felt that Oliver should return strictly to boyish pursuits
while others agreed that he should continue to dance "because he
wanted to." However, when asked what they would do in Oliver's
place, the responses of the boys changed. Up to now, judgements
were being made for a fictional storybook character; suddenly, the
decisions were being made based on personal likes and dislikes in
conjunction with their moral interpretation of right and wrong.
Many boys who were previously willing to let Oliver do as he
wanted, either stated that they would give up dancing in favour of
sports, or totally denied their own involvement, unable to even
conceptualize taking dancing lessons. Kennard attributes this difference in response to the position that the reader assumes from the
text, accepting the position of the central character during the
reading but then using that experience to say "This is what I am
not."[9] Overall, the evidence in this study suggests that, although
exposure to non-conventional roles in literature may be a catalyst
for encouraging children to explore their personal beliefs, when the
issues involve changing individual actions, children's views become
somewhat more tenuous.

When asked to explain why the non-conventional behaviours of
the storybook characters would be so unacceptable, responses again
varied widely. Several children discussed the possibility of actual
physical changes occurring to a boy who persists in doing girl
things.

Why do you think Oliver's dad doesn't want him to play girl things?
Because he don't want him to change into a girl.
Do you think that might happen, that he'd turn into a girl?
Yeah, because in a book I have it says if you watch too much TV you might turn into a TV. So if you do girl things you might turn into a girl.
Do you think that could ever happen?
Yeah. If boys played girl things for a long, long time, they'd probably turn into girls.
What if girls played boys things?
Then I guess they might turn into boys.   *Travis / 6*

John offered the same idea, but understood that actual physical changes were unlikely to occur, although in his opinion, what would happen was almost as serious.

What do you think will happen if Oliver keeps on dancing?
He'll turn into a girl. That happens in storybooks.
Would that ever happen in real life?
No, probably not. It's just pretend in storybooks.
But if he keeps on doing those things he'll be just like a girl.
Would that be okay, if he was like a girl?
No! No! No! Don't you understand? If people think you're a girl, that's just as bad as being one.   *John / 6*

Both Cathy and Leann rationalized that Oliver's non-conventional behaviour reflected negatively on the way other boys are perceived.

Do those other boys have to go to dancing school?
No. They never would.
Then why don't they want Oliver to go dancing?
Because they only do boys' stuff and they don't want him to do girls' stuff. They think he's a boy and he should do the same as them.
What if he doesn't do the same as them?
Well, the girls won't care but the boys won't like it because people might think they like dancing, too.   *Leann / 5*

Why did the other boys make fun of him and throw his shoes around?

Because they don't want him to be a big sissy.
Why wouldn't they just say "Go ahead and be a dancer. We don't care?"
Because if he does sissy things, then they would sorta be like a big sissy, too, because they're boys like him.
Would people think they like girl things, too?
Yeah, they'd think all boys were sissies. *Cathy / 6*

It was interesting to note the differing ways, based on their own personal beliefs and experiences, in which the children felt that society metes out consequences for deviant behaviours; teachers would send children to the principal, parents would ground them, coaches would kick them off teams, and peers would ridicule anyone who repeatedly transgressed.

Is it a good idea for Jesse to wear a skirt to school?
No, because he's a boy and the teacher would think he's a girl.
What would happen to him?
Well the other kids would probably laugh and then the teacher would send him to the principal. *Jill / 4*

What do you think would happen if Oliver keeps on playing girl games?
His dad would just kick him out the door.
So he couldn't live at home any more?
Not if he played girl games. He'd have to go to a girl house.
Jimmy / 5

The perceived consequences were usually in the form of punishment to the transgressor; the fact that Oliver's parents accepted his dancing at the book's conclusion could be successfully ignored in view of the children's expectations of what should happen or would happen to them under similar circumstances.

I found it surprising, however, that none of the children mentioned a need to change the rules about 'boy things' and 'girl things', simply accepting them as they understood them. In fact, when asked if they would stop doing an activity that elicited their peers' disapproval, most children reported that not only would they stop, but they would return to doing conventional boy or girl activities.

It may be that changing the rules is not perceived by children as being within their control. Or perhaps, they feel the anticipated consequences are too great to take the risk. The consistency of their responses indicates, however, that it will take repeated exposure to situations where non-conventional behaviours are accepted and celebrated in order to reduce the dissonance children feel. Fortunately for educators, overcoming such dissonance may also be the key to new learning.

Summarizing the Responses

After spending many hours in conversation with these children and subsequently analyzing their responses, I am left with several distinct impressions about children's understanding of gender. An overview of the responses to all four stories reveals that children seem to judge the acceptability of their actions against a set of tacit rules about appropriate behaviours for girls and boys. To children, these rules seem unchangeable, perhaps because their origin is unknown and the means by which they are enforced is unclear. However, it is evident from the data that children within this age range (four to six) have a sense of these rules and generally follow them, even if they are not always able to articulate them consistently to others.

Based on their understanding of what is acceptable for each sex, children tend to categorize behaviours as appropriate for 'girls only', 'boys only', or 'neutral—for both sexes'. The findings of this study show that, in classifying behaviours, children rely heavily on visible markers such as hair length, colour and style of clothing, make-up, jewellery, and hair adornments. The play behaviours most strongly associated with girls include doll play, low-contact sports, dancing, and dressing up. Block and vehicle play, high-contact sports, aggressive play, and the assumption of superhero roles are most commonly linked with boys.

As well, children's choice of peers is often sex-defined. Although the children within the study viewed mixed-sex play groupings as acceptable, most indicated a preference to play with same-sex peers, perpetuating the notion of sex-defined play activities. Their reasoning was based on the similar interests of same-sex friends. In describing control within mixed-sex groupings, both boys and girls perceived boys as being more dominant, which may account for girls' withdrawal to same-sex play situations.

When categorizing play behaviours as suitable for either a single sex or both sexes, it seems that the boundaries children construct are not always clearly defined. The differences depend upon each child's experiences in a variety of environments—with parents, teachers, peers, and the media providing the strongest influences. Involvement in play behaviours commonly associated with the opposite sex is acceptable under certain conditions; adult sanctioning, peer involvement, and a willingness to return to conventional sex-appropriate behaviours were the most commonly cited exceptions.

Thus, an understanding of the tacit rules of gendered play seems necessary for children to participate appropriately in the world of childhood. When conflicts arise in either understanding or negotiating these rules, children are forced to decide between doing what they want to do and doing what they feel they should do. Children's strongest fears about the consequences of inappropriate behaviour seem to be centred on their peer group's negative reaction; many children stated that they would change their behaviours if ridiculed by friends. However, because of children's experiences with power, they perceive adults as being the ones responsible for dealing with the inappropriate behaviours.

One impression I gained throughout the study was that children accept gender differences as they know them, perhaps because they do not yet conceive of other possibilities. Over and over again children stated that they like things the way they are now, that they are happy with the perceived differences between the ways boys and girls act, dress, and play. This is not surprising in view of the fact that children remain unaware of the social problems created by differing role expectations for males and females.

However, in seeking ways to motivate children to broaden their categories of appropriate gender behaviours, it is important to note that, although the children in the study did not seem to seek change actively, many of them were not totally adverse to it. In observing their reactions to non-conventional literature, although some children classified the conflicting information presented by the story-book characters as "wrong," modifying it to fit with their current beliefs, others responded more positively. It seemed that as the sessions progressed, with repeated exposure to non-conventional literature, some children were becoming more aware of the possibilities of a range of behaviours, and were beginning to consider change. This impression was supported by their classroom teachers, who commented that the children involved in the study raised gender-related issues more frequently, both during whole-class discussions and play activities.

The final impression I received was that, in spite of general agreement on many views, the children in the study were as different in the ways they perceived gender as the characters in the stories I presented to them. This is not surprising, considering that the children in this study differed in age, race, class, intelligence, degree of schooling, exposure to media, social play skills, and background experiences with gender issues—all contributing to their understanding of gender. Although the children's responses often seemed to separate them into two distinct groups, distinguished by biological sex, the differentiated knowledge the children brought to the problem-solving experience ensured their individuality. If there were such a thing as a scale to indicate children's conceptions of gender, then the children in this study would range from those viewing gender as a permanently-defined, unchangeable set of rules for boys and girls to those believing everyone should define their own rules about boys and girls. The variance in responses was one of the things which made my interactions with the children so rewarding, and at the same time suggested that we be judicious in whatever attempts we make to change the situation—the subject of the next three chapters.

5 / *Becoming Sensitive About Gender: The Children*

The analysis of the responses in the preceding chapters indicated that young children are not only developing definite views about acceptable gender roles, but are often unwilling to deviate from their beliefs. Since research suggests that sex-differentiated gender roles restrict educational opportunities for both girls and boys,[1] the findings imply not only that there is a definite need to increase awareness about how children view gender-related issues, but that it is necessary to find ways to modify undesirable patterns of behaviour being formed as a result of social upbringing. Since more educators seem willing to take up the challenge of broadening children's understanding of gender, the following chapters focus on ways the modification of educational programs and curricular content can address this need.

It is not an easy task to imagine an educational system devoid of the influences of gender. Because of the prevailing social emphasis on separate sex roles, educators must acknowledge that children do not and cannot grow up cultureless; children's conceptions of gender are necessarily influenced by the society in which they live. However, at the same time, we must not lose sight of the vision of an educational system which is free from the inequities of gender bias. The establishment of educational programs which recognize and strive to eliminate these inequities may be the first step towards a society which values sexual equality for both children and adults.

In examining the role of gender in education, Houston suggests that in order to free ourselves from potentially harmful gender bias, we must first become sensitive about gender itself, deliberately paying attention "when it can either prevent sex bias or further sex equality." Such a gender-sensitive perspective focusses on developing an awareness of how gender influences thinking by prompting us to monitor gender interactions and to intervene when necessary to equalize opportunities. "It encourages one to ask constantly: Is gender operative here? How is gender operative? What other effects do our strategies for eliminating gender bias have?"[2] Adopting a gender-sensitive perspective in the education of young children would thus necessitate our focussing on gender interactions within classrooms. We need to explore ways in which children, teachers—and the curriculum they implement together—can focus on the issue of becoming sensitive about gender.

There seems to be little doubt that, from the perspective of the children, gender is already operative in the world of childhood. The children's responses suggest that they are already developing definite views about acceptable gender roles, views which influence their style of dress, choice of toys, selection of play activities, and overall behaviour within the classroom setting. In fact, the findings of the study show that children make sense of gender by developing a set of tacit rules about how gender operates within their childhood world. By approaching gender from the children's point of view, we can come to understand why children think certain behaviours are appropriate for one sex and inappropriate for the other. Furthermore, by exploring the ways that children's developing conceptions of gender roles affect educational programming, educators can begin to devise strategies to eliminate harmful gender bias in educational programs for young children.

In developing new concepts or in broadening concepts they already possess, children would be encouraged to think about issues in challenging ways and to make decisions based on the information they receive. In relation to gender, instead of merely accepting children's current conceptions of gender roles and the resulting play behaviours, educators must be willing to challenge children on gender-related issues, encouraging them to explore and critically evaluate their current understanding of the concept. However, it must be recognized that there is a conflict between the way in which children are socialized and an educational program designed to create independent thinkers. For example, recent research (summarized in Appendix B) shows how the peer group, the family, and the media reinforce sex-defined roles—information which may conflict with that being presented by the gender-conscious classroom teacher.

Although researchers have suggested ways to counter the opposing messages provided by these external influences, the present discussion will zero in upon two considerations essential in helping young children develop an understanding of gender roles—the development of critical thinking about gender-related issues and the involvement of children as active agents in their own learning. Each of these will be discussed briefly as it applies to educational programs for young children.

Thinking Critically About Gender

In order to encourage children to think critically about gender, opportunities must first be provided within the classroom program for children to develop an awareness of gender as it currently operates in society. Enlightening the students about *how* things are is not enough; we need to discover ways to encourage children to think critically about *why* things are the way they are. Gaskell, McClaren & Novogrodsky discuss developing conscious awareness in terms of talking *with* students as opposed to talking *at* students, giving them "a sense of active and cooperative participation that equips them to engage in the struggle for social change."[3]

But is it possible to develop a sense of conscious awareness of gender issues in children as young as four years of age? Although some researchers may question the advisability of addressing gender concepts while the children are still sorting out role expectations, I maintain that these developing expectations are the reason gender roles *must* be explored at this age-level. Because the early childhood years are a critical time for children's learning, a time when they are attempting to make sense of the world around them, this is also the time when information about role behaviours for females and males will have a significant impact. Why wait until the child associates fixed stereotypic behaviours with boys and girls before trying to broaden their understanding of gender roles?

Furthermore, because we live in a literate society saturated with media images which focus on the differences between males and females instead of the similarities, children are constantly being bombarded by conflicting stimuli. For example, responses in this study show that these children recognized that the powerful, save-the-world Ninja Turtle superheroes are represented only as males, while the weak, powerless victims to be saved are represented as either females or small children. Davies suggests that since young children are already developing an awareness of women's subordination through these sexually-biased media images, educators can no longer afford to ignore the issue of gender.[4]

Children As Active Agents in Learning

A second recommendation is that educational programs acknowledge children as active agents in their own learning about gender relations, subsequently encouraging and valuing the knowledge that they acquire independently. As educators, if it is our intention to help children develop appropriate strategies to cope within an inequitably-gendered society without being restricted by it, we must not only encourage the children to take on the responsibility for developing their own understanding of gender, but must also learn to accept and value their findings in this area.

Unfortunately, one of the social expectations of childhood is that children will be the passive recipients of information transmitted by authority figures, generally teachers and parents. Such customs, which regard the adult as 'knowledge giver' and the child as 'knowledge receiver', imply power differentials which may be harmful to children.[5] Furthermore, because acceptable behaviours associated with the labels of 'boy' and 'girl' are handed down from parents, children are seldom encouraged to experiment with new role behaviours in order to develop their own concepts about gender. The result is that the knowledge about gender that children gain independently through active exploration of their world often becomes invisible in the presence of adult knowledge, or is sufficiently devalued to be considered unimportant.

The practice of accepting adult knowledge as 'valid' and the subsequent devaluation of children's knowledge must change if we hope to encourage children to develop their own understanding of gender roles. Anyone who has ever watched young children at play knows that children's minds are constantly at work discovering solutions to the problems that they face. Children talk easily and ask questions about gender behaviours, willingly explore gender roles through their fantasy play, and seldom hesitate to tell each other if a behaviour is strictly 'for girls' or 'for boys'.

The children participating in this study were no exception; their discussions revealed that they were eager to make sense of gender, making an active effort to determine what delineated the categories of boys and girls. The introduction of new, often conflicting, information to a category caused them to think and rethink their current conceptions, to weigh the conflicting information against what they already knew, and to either deny the evidence or adjust their current understanding to allow a better fit. Although admittedly children's ways of thinking may be faulty because of their lack of experience, these are nonetheless children's ways of thinking, and, as such, must be valued as an initial step in the process of developing an awareness of gender.

The importance of encouraging children to take an active, thinking role in developing their own understanding of gender cannot be overemphasized if we hope to create classrooms which are free from potentially damaging gender bias. How, then, can this knowledge be translated into classroom practice?

For very young children, the process of becoming aware of the influences of gender begins by encouraging children to talk about their understanding of the differences between 'boys' and 'girls'. Differing opinions and ideas, even if raised by the teacher, will evoke critical thinking if only through disagreement. These discussions will help children to learn to differentiate between role behaviours determined by biological sex and those formed through social expectations.

During a unit on babies in my Junior Kindergarten classroom, children were asked to discuss how they could differentiate between boy babies and girl babies. Answers ranged from girls being born with bows in their hair to the colour of the baby's clothing, but no child was willing to voice biological differences even after genital differences were pointed out on anatomical dolls. Following that discussion, however, several children were later observed in the hospital-centre talking about the fact that the baby was a boy even though he was wearing a dress. In light of examples such as these, change does appear possible given opportunities for group discussion, adult input, and sufficient motivation.

The point to be noted here is that without the initial discussions which are geared to find out what children actually think about gender-related issues, and the means by which they arrive at this knowledge, we cannot hope to expand children's thinking in other directions. Both children and teachers need to recognize the value of open-ended discussions about gender-related issues, discussions which result from issues raised intentionally through the curriculum or unintentionally in response to classroom incidents. Why are there fewer female police officers in books or on television? Do you think the Easter Bunny is a girl or a boy? Do you think the dog on the front of the book is a female or a male and what makes you think that? Who do you think can run faster, boys or girls? Questions such as these will evoke extended discussions amongst young children without ever arriving at any definite conclusion. Not only the choice of question but the way it is handled during the discussion is important; the teacher takes on the role of facilitator, making it clear that there may not be a correct answer, and when necessary, draws the discussion towards the opposing argument.

Children's informal interactions within the classroom setting can also be utilized to initiate discussions about gender. In my classroom, an incident in which one child told a boy wearing a gold chain that boys don't wear necklaces inspired an impromptu trip around the school to see how many male staff members and students wore jewellery. By being available to hear the comment, the teacher was able to expand upon it in a way that the children might not have done independently. Although children regularly discuss conflicting views, it is helpful if an adult is willing to extend these conflicts into classroom discussions so that more than just two children will benefit from the knowledge gained.

Another suggestion is for the teacher deliberately to create classroom situations which draw children's attention towards gender. In my classroom, removing all of the literature written by male authors for a two-week period forced the children to recognize that many of their favourite books were authored by males, particularly when a desired book was unavailable. This simple action and the accompanying discussions encouraged the children to pay attention to the sex of the author. Upon realizing that both men and women authored books, the children began to question whether the books we read daily were written by a woman or a man. Although this seems like a simple realization for young children to make, the situation inadvertently led to a focus on the sex of the characters in the story, and resulted in discussions about whether opposite-sex characters would behave in a similar fashion.

From these examples, it becomes apparent that there is no universal plan for ensuring success in developing gender awareness amongst young children. The strategies proposed are situationally dependent, occurring within a single classroom context in which the children and the teacher work together. It is important to re-emphasize, however, that the success of any strategy is dependent on its potential to encourage the children to think critically, while allowing them an active resolution of the problem through participation and discussion. Paying attention to gender is something children must learn to do independently. The responsibility for implementing these strategies most often rests with the classroom teacher, whose role we address in the next chapter.

6 / Becoming Sensitive About Gender: The Teacher

Developing an Understanding of Gender Influences

In order for teachers to understand how gender operates within the classroom environment and make the necessary program adjustments to encourage change, they must first be prepared to explore their own personal understanding of gender. To do this, teachers need to begin thinking about how gender is presently constituted in their own lives, as well as to recall instances where gender has influenced their own upbringing and schooling. By recognizing how they became 'gendered' persons, in the sense we have been using that term throughout, teachers ought to be in a better position to analyze how gender influences the lives of their pupils, and thus to develop a clearer understanding of how, and to what degree, gendered classroom practices affect sexual equality and educational equity.

Because many teachers of young children are women, it is particularly important that they realize how their own gendered behaviours can influence teacher expectations and classroom practices, in addition to affecting the way that students will respond to them. Research studies confirm that early childhood education classrooms are very feminine places, and that, out of a concern to achieve their own traditional femaleness, female teachers are more likely to reward 'femininity' in dress, actions and nurturing behaviours.[1] Although most girls willingly accept and follow this feminine model, the boys in the classroom are more likely to rebel against it out of a need to redefine their maleness. Immersed in what they view as a traditionally female environment, boys often respond aggressively, seizing control of their play and refusing to allow the girls entry into it.[2] This claim may help to explain not only why the boys in this study perceived themselves as controlling girls' entry into their play, but why the girls meekly allowed the boys to do so. Whereas, for the girls, a feminine world seems both acceptable and desirable, the boys appear to reaffirm their masculinity by actively demonstrating power over others.

Davies also notes how differing interactive styles adopted by boys and girls can affect their ability to learn within the classroom setting. By assuming a rebellious, aggressive style, not only do boys force increased interaction with the teacher, but their approach to learning becomes more independent and autonomous. The converse is true for girls; in accepting teacher requirements for silence, neatness and conformity, girls may resign themselves to a more passive learning process, becoming teacher-pleasers and avoiding taking unnecessary risks.[3] Whether such distinctions actually affect specific learnings, however, was not a question raised in this study and obviously one that requires much additional research.

The findings here *do* show that children are aware of the differences between the play styles of girls and boys, both within the classroom setting and on the playground. Several children noted that whereas boys got into trouble more often and were more disobedient, girls worked harder, got things done faster, and were generally better students. The children's understanding of the ways that boys and girls consistently differ in toy preferences, acceptable forms of sport and dance, and involvement in aggressive play also shows that young children are conscious of differing interactive and learning styles for the two sexes, an awareness which probably guides the 'correctness' of their own activity choices. It seems unlikely, however, that at this age level, children consciously see their decisions as being influenced by their teacher's expectations.[4]

Although the differences in the way that boys and girls play cannot be totally attributed to the 'femininity' portrayed by their traditionally female teachers, this does seem to be a contributing factor. Studies suggest that gender considerations feature prominently in the way teachers define both themselves and their classroom practices. Both male and female teachers therefore need to remain aware of the potential implications, for children's under-standing of gender roles, of both the teacher's biological sex and the gendered behaviours exhibited within the classroom setting.

There seems to be no simple solution to this problem. Few male teachers are willing to work in the primary grades, a traditionally female sphere. Furthermore, arbitrarily increasing the number of male teachers in primary programs may have adverse or unforeseen effects on girls. A more feasible solution may be to encourage teachers of both sexes to examine carefully their own feelings about the traditional feminine and masculine behaviours displayed by children in their own classrooms, and to monitor closely their own expectations for such behaviours.

Monitoring Teaching Practices

Along with an analysis of their own genderedness, it is important that teachers carefully examine their teaching practices for the pre-sence of stereotyped behaviours. Is the language modelled within the classroom deliberately gender neutral? The use of terms such as 'policeman' or 'fireman' may be restricting children's concep-tions of acceptable occupations for men and women. Are children labelled or grouped based on biological sex? The continual use of the labels 'girls' and 'boys', as opposed to the more encompassing term 'children', may inadvertently cause students to focus on dif-ferences between the sexes. Is teacher time equitably divided bet-ween boys and girls? Additional time spent with boys, even if neg-ative in intent, may cause boys to view themselves as more important and girls to view themselves as inconsequential. Are certain toys, activities, or behaviours reinforced as being more appropriate for one sex than the other? Children may be developing notions that certain actions are sex-defined and thus inappropriate for the opposite sex. Are both mixed-sex and same-sex play encouraged through classroom set-up, toy selection, and teacher presence? Children who play continuously with peers of the same sex may unintentionally be developing sex-differentiated behaviours, which in turn may prove harmful to their development.

Teachers will need constant motivation and support in their endeavours to initiate change. Whether in the form of a teaching partner who is also attempting to change stereotyped practices, or a support group made up of teachers who meet together on a regular basis for discussion and analysis of programs, teachers must be prepared to provide assistance and support for one another. The development of inservice programs—to instruct teachers in ways to recognize sexual bias within teaching practices, curricular content, and the behaviours of the children themselves—may be one step towards encouraging teachers to become critically aware of their own classroom practices. The development of a checklist of sex-stereotyped teaching practices to be avoided may also prove helpful. Regular assessment of classroom events through video and audio recording will assist teachers to focus on those teaching practices which need modification. It is only by constantly monitoring their own classroom practices that teachers will learn to repeatedly seek out answers for two important questions: "Does gender matter in this situation?" and, if so, "How can teaching practices be changed to address the problem?"

Sharing Control in the Classroom

Some researchers imply that the teacher's philosophy about how children learn, and more specifically, the way control is maintained within the classroom setting, can also influence children's understanding of gender roles and the resultant degree of gender bias in the classroom.[5] Berk & Lewis suggest that a classroom setting that places the teacher in authority and emphasizes direct instruction promotes higher incidence of sex-typed behaviours and same-sex peer interaction because gender roles are viewed as being separate and unalterable. By contrast, in a classroom which promotes shared, interactive control between the children and the teacher, a wider spectrum of activities is considered acceptable for both sexes because the gender roles are less strictly defined.[6]

Davies attributes these differences to children's experiences with power,[7] suggesting that in classrooms in which the teacher is perceived as the sole authority figure, children are learning to accept rather than question power differentials in human relations.

> To the extent that teachers' interactions with their pupils are based on a display of their power, then they are teaching children to accept power differentials in human relations as normative and are providing detailed interactive knowledge which can be used to sustain power relations across both class and gender. (p. 15)

Young children's recognition and acceptance of power differentials, particularly between adults and children, was also evident in the findings of my study. Based on their consistent exposure to powerful adults at home, at school and on television, children repeatedly assigned powerful roles to God, teachers, principals, parents and coaches. Many children also perceived fathers as being more powerful than mothers, and men as being more powerful than women, based on the male-associated traits of greater strength, speed and size.

When viewed collectively, these findings suggest that the methods by which teachers establish the power balance within their classrooms may have a significant impact on children's understanding of gender. A classroom in which power is shared between teacher and students may encourage children to question the power differentials they encounter daily in other settings, simply because of the discord created through exposure to differing environments. Teachers must not only become aware of the imbalance of power in adult-child and boy-girl relationships and its potential for harm, but must also seek out ways to foster collaboration among all members of the classroom community in order to provide a more democratic environment and a more equitable model for future social practice.

It is apparent that the attitudes and expectations which teachers and children develop together about gendered behaviours are an essential element in the reduction of inequitable gender bias. Moreover, it is important that these changing attitudes be developed and enforced through the educational materials and curricular content being taught. In other words, steps must be taken to ensure that the curriculum itself is gender-sensitive.

7 / Becoming Sensitive About Gender: The Curriculum

The term 'curriculum' is assigned a variety of meanings in the educational literature, ranging from Pratt's "prescribed content of study with formal educational or training intentions" to Johnson's "a teacher-student negotiated series of learning outcomes."[1] Differences in definitions largely depend on how the control of curricular decisions is assigned, and whether ownership rests with the Ministry of Education, the school administration, the teacher, the students, or varying combinations of these.

In many contemporary educational programs for young children, much of the learning is based on the children's independent choice of activities, and assumes that the children themselves will take on the responsibility for their own learning outcomes. A definition of curriculum within this kind of classroom must therefore encompass the content which children learn from the chosen activities and the processes through which they acquire knowledge, and include as well the teacher's role in helping children to achieve curricular goals. In this context, the term 'curriculum' refers to the complete program of activities negotiated between teacher and students to meet prescribed educational ends or objectives.[2]

Assuming that the establishment of learning situations which are free from harmful gender bias is a desired educational outcome, then certain modifications will need to be made to the program of activities offered to young children. Although it is difficult to separate an integrated curriculum into its constituent elements, the goal of developing an awareness of the need for gender equality—among teachers and students—will be discussed with regard to three closely connected curricular areas: the selection of children's literature, structured circle activities, and play situations and toy selection.

The Selection of Children's Literature

Children's literature—in conjunction with the poetry, storytelling, puppetry, and drama which spring from it—is an essential part of the school curriculum for young children, functioning to support and extend the children's developing language base. Picture books are a valued means by which children learn about societal and cultural values; through exposure to what other boys and girls do and say and feel, children come to generalize what is expected of them in similar situations. The story characters become their role models, setting standards against which children can measure their own behaviours, or providing a glimpse of the future into which they will grow. Because most children encounter literature at a time when they are developing gender identity, it is important that they be exposed to print materials that represent gender fairly. This implies including stories which present children of *both* sexes involved in a *variety* of roles, as well as providing literature written by both male and female authors.

Unfortunately, much of the reading material readily available to young children continues to be a source of gender bias. The majority of story characters in literature, whether represented as humans, fantasy characters, or animated animals are male, promoting the underlying message that males are important and females are insignificant by comparison. Those stories which do include both male and female characters, most often portray the male characters as active, independent and generally competent, while the females are viewed as passive, dependent and incompetent.[3]

Although Petersen & Lach (1990) found gender bias to be less prevalent in picture books published since 1987, citing more equal representation of females in increasingly dominant roles, the researchers are careful to point out that the differences are not significant. Although the recent publishing trend to promote stories which feature powerful female protagonists and to reward female authorship is encouraging, it is unlikely that all new books being published will be free of gender stereotypes. Furthermore, many children may never encounter these recent books. Although ministries of education often monitor the content of basal reading series made available to school systems, the same controls do not apply to children's literature, even though books are an essential part of the primary curriculum. As a result, decisions about individual picture books remain largely with school librarians and classroom teachers. Since research shows that in selecting literature for children both teachers and parents rely heavily on "personal favourites"[4] from their own childhood, children's reading material may remain stereotyped in spite of recent publications. How, then, can educators realistically resolve the problem of inequitable gender representation prevalent in children's literature?

First, it is important that teachers present children with much literature that is free from obvious and potentially distorting gender bias—to provide both a standard of comparison and to allow children to see a range of potential roles. Children of all ages need to be exposed to literature which portrays women as valued creators of history; as strong, intelligent protagonists; as controllers of their own behaviours. They need to hear stories about men who are dependent on others, nurturant care-givers, and empathetic listeners. These are the stories which draw children's focus to the similarities between girls and boys, men and women instead of the differences.

The literature used in my study, selected to encourage children to talk about gender, falls within this category, presenting child-characters engaged in behaviours which are viewed by children as being non-conventional for their biological sex. Stories which present girls who would rather climb trees than play with dolls, or boys who prefer dancing over football, encourage children to question and discuss the acceptability of traditional play activities, if only through overt rebellion against the behaviour of the story characters. Zipes attributes the success of stories such as these to their ability to disturb the ways of thinking that children traditionally accept; by questioning the behaviours of the story characters, children are also forced to examine their own behaviours.[5] It is hoped that with continued exposure to behaviours which are discordant with children's ways of thinking, that children will broaden their own view of role potentiality, thereby extending the conceptual framework that they are developing about the limits of gendered behaviour.

Although it makes sense theoretically to limit children's choice of reading materials to those books designated free from gender bias, in practice, this seems unrealistic. Children and teachers need to be able to make curricular choices from a wide selection of literature. Not only would it be a mammoth task to cull all inappropriate books from a school library, but, with current budget restrictions, reading materials would become severely limited. Furthermore, it is unlikely that educational personnel would ever agree upon appropriate standards for the elimination of a particular book, and the issue of political censorship of children's reading materials would be raised by many interested parties. Assuming that reading materials could be limited within the school environment, teachers would still have no control over the literature accessible to children within the home or through public libraries.

A more practical solution is for teachers and students to apply an awareness of gender stereotyping to the materials they select for classroom use. By acknowledging the profound influences that books can and do have on children's affective and cognitive development, teachers can utilize books as a teaching tool to develop children's own awareness of gender stereotyping. Instead of simply eliminating all books which display stereotypes, teachers can focus on the stereotyping within specific books, encouraging children to seek out and recognize bias within the literature that they read and to think out necessary changes.

With encouragement and practice, children as young as four years of age are able to recognize and discuss stereotypes within literature, as we have seen in this study. Children can be encouraged to count the number of male and female characters, and discuss how the story would change if the sex of the characters were different. They can learn to examine critically character types according to the clothing they wear, the toys they play with, the formation of their peer groups, and the roles they perform, and to determine how these activities are influenced by gender. Many young children can predict how the story would change if roles were reversed or if the protagonists were of the opposite sex. They can imagine themselves taking the place of both same-sex and opposite-sex story characters and the possibilities that would result. With continued exposure to a variety of literature, children will come to realize that persons of both sexes can author and illustrate books.

Structured Circle Activities

In addition to print materials, the activities shared during a structured circle-time most often include a variety of songs, poems, finger plays, and games—derived from the culture of childhood. Because many of these activities have been handed down from generation to generation, they are usually saturated with male characters and masculine pronouns, often presenting traditional images of males in powerful, dominant roles and females in powerless, submissive ones. A sampling of children's favourite nursery rhymes, songs, and games produces an extensive list of popular male characters such as Humpty Dumpty, Rudolf, Santa Claus, Peter Cottontail, Mr. Sun, Frosty the Snowman, and the Grand Old Duke of York. Female characters are conspicuously absent, and those in- cluded are most often presented in traditional roles, as frightened little girls who run from spiders, submissive wives who are kept in pumpkin shells, and old women whose sole existence is caring for children and pets.

How, then, can a curriculum, historically rooted in a patriarchal culture, ensure equal representation of both male and female figures? Faced with the repercussions of ignoring children's cultural language heritage by eliminating all activities which are deemed sexist, the modification of traditional songs, poems, and games seems preferable. Children who have only ever sung the version of 'The Farmer in the Dell' which includes a male farmer and a female wife may initially rebel at an altered version which asks a female or male farmer to select a friend; however, the discussion which evolves from the change will assist in developing the children's awareness of extended possibilities for male and female roles. Similarly, changing the words in order to sing about 'Mrs. Sun' or 'Frosty the Snowwoman' seems inconsequential; however, such simple changes which focus children's attention on gendered language labels will help increase awareness about the need for equal representation of males and females.

Because the domination of male figures in childhood activities is culturally acceptable, the responsibility for initiating change once again rests with the teacher. Hopefully, exposure to the original versions of the activities along with discussions of the need for change can be used to encourage critical thinking amongst children while reinforcing the need for gender equality. As one four-year-old girl in my classroom pointed out to a supply teacher, "You've just gotta sing about Mrs. Sun to make it fair."

Play Situations and Toy Selection

A common objective of educational programs for young children is to provide them with play situations that will encourage the development of relationships with others. Thus, in addition to facilitating the development of specific motor and cognitive skills, toys are provided which will increase the likelihood of developing such social skills as cooperation with others, verbalization of problems, and fair negotiation of solutions.

Since, in childhood, knowledge is constructed through experiential play, in order for girls and boys to develop similar skills, it is essential that children of both sexes have equal access to all toys. However, the findings of this study show that not only do most young children categorize many of their favourite toys as being suitable for a single sex, but they prefer to socialize with same-sex friends, forming play groups in conjunction with their preferred toys. Since continuous same-sex groupings are likely to further reinforce sex-defined roles, it becomes necessary to promote toy selections and play situations which will facilitate both mixed-sex play (boys and girls playing together) and cross-sex play (boys playing with 'girl' toys and girls playing with 'boy' toys).

Although one obvious solution is to provide only 'neutral' toys, eliminating all toys which children strongly associate with one sex or the other, this practice is adult-controlled and fails to encourage children to develop an understanding of the reasons behind their play choices. If we hope to promote behaviours that will be generalized and transferred outside of the classroom setting, it is not enough to tell children not to do something; they must learn to think critically about why things are the way they are, and make appropriate choices based on their acquired knowledge. Furthermore, although the rationale for removing toys which promote sex-stereotyped media images, such as superhero figures or Barbie dolls, may be clear, it is much harder to justify the removal of such sex-typed toys as baby dolls, vehicles, or blocks, all of which encourage fantasy roles, and creative and manipulative play.

A more appropriate solution is to introduce all toys through the use of demonstration models of both sexes, along with the message that support and encouragement will be provided for all children who choose to play with a particular toy. Both cross-sex and mixed-sex toy play can be increased by teacher presence and support at specific centres, by teacher modelling of play with gender-specific toys, and through selective reinforcement of desired play behaviours.

Open discussion about why girls and boys seldom play together or why children prefer specific toys can also be helpful in encouraging children to choose a variety of activities. When mixed-sex play situations result in disagreement, children need to be urged to solve the problem verbally. A class discussion about why the boys don't want the girls to play with them at blocks, or why the girls don't want the boys invading the house-centre, raises gender consciousness by dealing directly with the issues of equality and fairness, without requiring adult control through the 'teacher made me do it' syndrome. Hopefully, the use of discussions to explore and reinforce the similarities between children will result in decreased or unwarranted emphasis on the biological differences between boys and girls.

Continued exposure to literature which presents characters involved in non-conventional play behaviours in a positive manner may also help children rethink their acceptance of traditional play patterns and toys. Their current contacts encouraging single-sex play are numerous; media picturing girls in frilly dresses and boys in rugged clothes promoting toys specific to one sex or the other, parents who buy dolls for girls and baseball bats for boys before they are even able to walk, and peers who say "Don't play that. That's a sissy girl toy!" or "You'll get dirty playing football!" all present single-sex play as 'normal' and therefore appropriate behaviour. Through its conflicting view, non-conventional literature may thus become an additional means of presenting children with acceptable alternatives and promoting related discussion.

Afterword

It seems apparent that much of the responsibility for reducing gender bias within the education system continues to rest with teachers. If we hope to elicit change, we must find ways to empower both teachers and children to become active agents in their own learning about gender relations, to judge how our own genderedness affects both the children we teach and the classroom practices we enforce and to ensure that the curriculum not only be free of harmful gender bias, but simultaneously help students develop an awareness of the current social inequalities between males and females. In the face of such a mammoth task, the place to begin developing a sensitivity about gender appears to be through educational programs for young children.

One of the problems that both teachers and researchers face is uncertainty about which solutions are the most appropriate. The relationship between education and the gender roles of young children is largely uncharted territory and as a result, we do not know the results of long-term attempts to change attitudes. In trying to find solutions, we are currently evaluating the information of reflective practitioners, informed classroom teachers who are utilizing trial-and-error methods to determine the effects of gender-sensitive classroom practices in studies such as this one. Because these observations reflect real children and actual classroom programs, the conclusions they make about gender stereotyping may be the most valid of all.

In attempting to pay attention to gender stereotyping, it is easy to recommend classroom practices which will change the superficial attitudes of children; for children learn very quickly in our society that to parrot the words adults wish to hear earns them rewards, recognition and advancement. It is far more difficult, however, to institute classroom practices which will develop conscious awareness in children about gender roles. This requires programs which empower children—by treating them as individuals, by listening to them and encouraging the negotiation of meanings and intentions, by providing opportunities for them to assume control of their own learning. These will be the children who, as adults, will have the power, the wisdom and the courage to change society.

It is not an easy task we ask of teachers. To value and implement these types of programs, teachers must first understand the complex role that gender plays within the social order of our culture. They must recognize the confining nature of sex-differentiated roles for children of both sexes and the harm that is being done to children through the power imbalance in classrooms. They must be willing to institute change within their own lives that will be reflected in their teaching practices.

In spite of the difficulty of the task, the long-term rewards will make it worthwhile. For if we can envision a classroom where being a child is more important than being a boy or a girl, then the vision of a society which values being a person more highly than being male or female becomes clearer. As educators, we must remember that the possibilities for change remain with the children that we teach. They must be the ones to own the vision.

Notes

Notes for Chapter One

1. See, for example, Best, 1983; Davies, 1988; Pitcher & Schultz, 1983; Spender, 1989; Spender & Sarah, 1980; Stacey, Bereaud & Daniels, 1974; and Walkerdine, 1984. More detailed and specific references are given throughout the book.
2. See Bruce, 1985, p. 49.
3. For a discussion of language and gender schema see Money & Tucker, 1975, p. 116. Holdaway (1979) and Jaggar & Smith-Burke (1985) are important sources for understanding early literacy behaviours.
4. See Garnica, 1979; Gleason, 1979; and Money & Tucker, 1975.
5. See Zipes, 1982 and Davies, 1989c.

Notes for Chapter Two

1. For further discussion, see Rosen, 1986.
2. Favat (1977), quoted in Davies, 1989c, p. 43.
3. Zipes, 1982; both quotations appear on p. 322.
4. For a discussion of the social pressures that underlie early gender-role formation, see Davies, 1988, 1989c; Intons-Peterson, 1988; and Money & Tucker, 1975.
5. Davies (1989c) and Zipes (1982) discuss, in particular, the liberating role of fairy tales. Aitken (1988) discusses the importance of fairy tales in general as well as within a feminist context.
6. See Harste, Woodward & Burke (1984) for a discussion of children as active constructors of knowledge and Davies (1989c) for an analysis of children's changing perceptions of gender.
7. The research design selected for this study drew upon, amongst others, the naturalistic paradigm (Lincoln & Guba, 1982, 1985), illuminative

evaluation (Parlett & Hamilton, 1977), participant observation and experiential analysis (Reinharz, 1979), and qualitative field research (Patton, 1980). Although the nomenclature and procedures differ, the commonality shared by these researchers is their assumption of increased validity of a qualitative design over one which is quantitative in nature. This increased validity is largely the result of techniques utilized for evaluation, including an analysis of observable recurrent patterns of behaviour, and an emphasis on observational inference (Lincoln & Guba, 1985).

8. See, for example, Parlett & Hamilton, 1977.
9. I had been the Junior Kindergarten teacher for all of the children involved in the study. Their familiarity with my role as teacher was extended through program integration, as the children in Grade One and Senior Kindergarten were continually returning to the Junior Kindergarten room to share stories, art work and dramatic presentations.
10. See Davis, 1987; Schacher, 1976; and Wilms & Cooper, 1987.
11. Patton, 1980, p. 122.
12. *Ibid.*, p. 123.
13. There are many accounts of the best way to analyze data in qualitative research. I found Reinharz (1979) particularly persuasive; she describes a process called "experiential analysis" in which both the experiences of the children and the researcher become a valued part of the knowledge gained. "The researcher engages, collaborates, lets happen, questions, follows, not knowing the outcome in advance. Such an attitude is crucial lest the researcher waste the opportunity for learning from the natural situation by imposing on it external categories to which his or her attention is directed" (p. 357). Reading about experiential analysis and questioning its place within the present study made me more cognizant of reflecting on my changing role as researcher. Since the process of analyzing data was ongoing throughout the response sessions, I realized that not only was the study helping me to gain a better understanding of my role as researcher, but I was simultaneously becoming more proficient at it. Throughout the entire process, however, I continued to wonder whether or not I was analyzing the data in 'the right way'. I was reassured by Patton's (1980, p. 299) remarks: "The analysis of qualitative data is a creative process. It is also a process of intellectual rigor and a great deal of hard work. Because different people manage their creativity, intellectual endeavours, and hard work in different ways, there is no right way to

go about organizing, analyzing, and interpreting qualitative data. Each qualitative analyst must find his or her own process."

Notes for Chapter Three

1. See Intons-Peterson, 1988; Kessler & McKenna, 1978; Pitcher & Schultz, 1983; and Davies, 1987.
2. Intons-Peterson, 1988, p. 85.
3. Kessler & McKenna, 1978, p. 164.
4. Carlsson-Paige & Levin, 1990, p. 92.
5. *Ibid.*, the evolution of 'Barbie' and 'Jem' are cited as typical examples. "The focus of all these dolls is on clothes, hairstyles and make-up which reflect the latest fashions of the glamorous and affluent. 'Mattel', the manufacturer of the Barbie toy line claims to be the world's largest producer of 'women's wear' today. One standard for beauty is imported to girls through such toys, and no real diversity in terms of ethnicity or body type....Each series has a lead doll who is sexy and thin and usually blond. One or two dolls have darker skin and hair, but otherwise, all the dolls closely resemble the lead doll."
6. *Ibid.*
7. For a detailed discussion see Bredmeier, Shields, Weiss & Cooper, 1986; Kidd, 1987; and Monagan, 1983.
8. Bredmeier *et al.*, *ibid.*, p. 314.
9. See Monagan, 1983, pp. 61-62. The quotation from Rainer Martens appears on p. 62. The fragile state of the male ego, particularly in the area of sport, is supported by further research findings which show that when boys lose, they attribute their failure to bad luck, whereas girls equate losses with either their own lack of skill or their opponents' superior skills. See Iso-ahola, 1979; Monagan, 1983; and Nichols, 1975.
10. See Iso-ahola, 1979.
11. Carlsson-Paige & Levin (1990) connect violent play images, in the present study described only by boys, to the marketing strategies of the war toys with which children play. They suggest that war toys demand the use of power and violence through the media images they represent and the toy owners (most often boys) respond by playing in a violent, aggressive manner.
12. See Davies, 1982, p. 76.
13. Differences in the degree of aggression apparent here in the responses of the girls and the boys are supported by Pitcher & Schultz (1983,

pp. 24, 25) who found that active forms of aggression (i.e., hitting) were more prevalent in three- to five-year-old boys while passive forms of aggression (i.e., withdrawal and ignoring) were more popular amongst girls of the same age.

14. McRobbie (1986, p. 134) says: "Social pressures...direct little girls towards dance as a suitably feminine form of leisure [for] dancing is linked with being pretty, graceful, controlled, and an object of admiration."

15. *Ibid.*, p. 143.

16. *Ibid.*, pp. 133 and 137. In citing this research I do not mean to imply here that young children view dance as a means of sexual expression. However, it is important to note that both boys and girls are already valuing the surface features of dancing—costumes, beauty, and movements, all characteristics that objectify the female body. None of them commented, for instance, that dancers have to be strong or agile or aerobically fit or even clever enough to remember the routines. Through exposure to popular dance films, such as *Dirty Dancing*, older children may already be realizing that dancing is one means through which women receive admiration from others in order to become socially desirable persons. This could prove problematic for girls who may simultaneously be learning that they will be loved for how they look and what they can do with their bodies rather than for who they are.

17. *Ibid.*, p. 134.

18. Davies, 1987, p. 46.

19. This polarization of role definitions is confirmed by Carlsson-Paige & Levin (1990, p. 42) who report that the division in play between the sexes is occurring at earlier ages. They attribute the earlier onset to stereotypic images portrayed by television programs and the toys that accompany them, through which strength, dominance, and competition are emphasized for boys, and relationships, feelings, and appearance are emphasized for girls. Other researchers suggest that there is value in children's defining such distinct differences in male-female roles through their fantasy play. Bettelheim (1975) maintains that children portray mothers within a domestic setting out of a desire to keep their own mothers at home as long as possible, thus strengthening the mother-child bond. Paley (1973) suggests that children enact the mother-baby relationship searching for the safe family environment it represents. However, neither of these researchers appears concerned that these roles, so distinctly separate in the dress-

up play of young children, continue to be perpetuated in society; they give no thought to how these roles might be implicated in the social problems of male violence, rape, and wife and child abuse. It appears that, as an indicator of children's developing understanding of gender roles, differences in the dress-up play of girls and boys will require further study and research.

Notes for Chapter Four.

1. See Pitcher & Schultz, 1983, p. 30. Further discussion may be found on p. 27.
2. *Ibid.*
3. Research by Bruce (1985) and Davies (1989c) confirms these findings, reporting that preschool boys verbally and physically abuse female classmates in order to remove them from what the boys define as their own play areas.
4. See Askew & Ross, 1988; Bruce, 1985; Carlsson-Paige & Levin, 1990; Davies, 1989c; and Pitcher & Schultz, 1983.
5. See MacLean, 1972 and Robinson, 1983.
6. See, for example, Walkerdine & Lucey, 1989.
7. Davies, 1988. It would be interesting to know, as well, more about how schoolchildren of both sexes respond to the 'power' of men teachers and women teachers, especially since most of their teachers in primary school are women.
8. See Davies, 1987 and Weitzman, 1979.
9. Kennard, 1986, p. 70.

Notes for Chapter Five.

1. See Best, 1983; Spender, 1989; Spender & Sarah, 1980; and Stacey *et al.*, 1974.
2. Houston, 1985, p. 365. The subsequent quotation is taken from p. 368.
3. Gaskell, McClaren & Novogrodsky, 1989, p. 38.
4. Davies, 1988.
5. According to some researchers (for example, Berk & Lewis, 1977) these differentials can be correlated with an increase in the incidence of sex-defined roles and gendered practices.

Notes for Chapter Six

1. See, for example, Campbell, 1987; Davies, 1988; and Evans, 1982.
2. See Davies, 1988, p. 23.
3. *Ibid.*
4. Walkerdine (1989, p. 257) takes the notion of teacher influence one step further, suggesting that female teachers remain on the outskirts of boys' play because they feel intimidated or are unable to identify with play patterns absent from their own childhood. She goes on to suggest that since boys portray the qualities that female teachers lack, teachers may subconsciously set out to develop the boys' potential while ignoring their female students (p. 267). Research showing that female teachers interact more with boys who are macho or intelligent, while failing to encourage intellectual girls, seems to support this theory; see Evans, 1982, p. 141.
5. See Davies, 1988 and Minuchin, 1976.
6. Berk & Lewis, 1977, pp. 214-215.
7. Davies (1988, p. 15) also intimates that the adult-child inequality in classrooms may be perceived by children as a prototype for male-female inequality, a thesis which requires further exploration within classroom settings.

Notes for Chapter Seven

1. See Pratt, 1980 and Johnson, 1967 for more details.
2. For a more complete discussion see Barrow, 1984, Chs. 1 and 3.
3. See Batcher, Brackstone, Winter & Wright, 1987; Freebody & Baker, 1985; Lobban, 1987; and Petersen & Lach, 1990. For a somewhat different view about the purpose and uses of the older, gender-biased legends and fairy tales, see Aitken, 1988.
4. See Petersen & Lach, 1990.
5. See Zipes, 1982.

Appendix A / Literature Response Questions

The following questions were developed as a guide to encourage the children to reveal their conceptions of gender through a discussion of the story. It was sometimes necessary to extend the children's answers through additional questions in response to the answers that they gave.

Questions for *The Paper Bag Princess*

1. Did you like the story? What part did you like best?
2. If you were Elizabeth and you woke up one day and found all your clothes burned off and your friends kidnapped by a dragon, what would you do? If you were Ronald, and you woke up one day and found out that you were being carried off by a dragon, what would you do?
3. Do you think that Elizabeth was very brave to go right up to the dragon and dare it to do things? Would you be brave enough to go right up to the dragon and dare it to do things? Who do you know that would be that brave? Who do you think was the bravest in the story, Elizabeth, Ronald, or the dragon?
4. Do you think that Elizabeth was very clever to find a way to trick the dragon? Do you think that you would be that clever? Who do you know that would be that clever? Who do you think was the cleverest in the story, Elizabeth, Ronald, or the dragon?
5. Do you think it was right of Ronald to tell Elizabeth that she was a mess? Should he have married her the way she looked? What should he have done?

6. Why do you think that Elizabeth called Ronald "a bum" at the end of the story? Should she have said that to him? What should she have done? If, the next day, Elizabeth came back clean and neat and dressed like at the beginning of the book, do you think that she should marry Ronald then?

7. What do you think is happening in this very last picture here? (*sunset picture*) What do you think that Elizabeth will do now? Where do you think she will go? Do you think that Elizabeth will live happily ever after? What will Ronald do? Do you think that Ronald will live happily ever after?

8. If you were Princess Elizabeth, would you love a prince like Ronald? If you were Prince Ronald, would you love a princess like Elizabeth?

9. Do you think that this story has a happy ending? Do you think that it should have ended this way? If you had written this story, how would you have made it end?

Questions for *Oliver Button Is a Sissy*

1. Did you like the story? What part did you like best?

2. What kinds of games do you like to play? Are there any games or toys that you think are just for boys? Just for girls?

3. Why do you think that Oliver Button didn't like to play boys' games? Was it okay for Oliver to do things like picking flowers and dancing? What kinds of things should he do? What kinds of things shouldn't he do?

4. What do you think it means to be a sissy? Why did Oliver's dad tell him not to be a sissy? Why do you think his dad didn't want Oliver to dance and play girls' games? Do you think that Oliver's dad was right to tell him not to play girls' games? At the end of the story, his dad doesn't mind his dancing any more now that he's a tap dancer. Why do you think that happened?

5. What do you think of the boys who tease Oliver? If those boys were your friends and they called Oliver a sissy, would you tease him, too? Was it okay to write "Oliver Button is a sissy" on the wall? Why do you think that Oliver keeps dancing, even though everyone teases him? If you were Oliver, and you really

loved to dance, would you keep on dancing even if everyone teased you?

6. Do you think that the boys and girls like Oliver at the end of the book? Who do you think wrote on the wall, "Oliver Button is a star?" Why did they change their minds? Do you think that it's okay for Oliver to do things like dancing and dressing up now? Would he still learn how to play football?

7. Is it okay for boys to do things that girls do? Is it okay for girls to do things that boys do? Do you know any boys who like to do girl things? Any girls who like to do boy things? How are they at doing them?

8. What would you have done if you were Oliver and everyone made fun of you for being different? What if one of your boy/girl (*same sex as child*) friends wanted to do a boy/girl (*opposite sex of child*) thing, would you do it with them? How do you think you'd feel?

9. Do you think that this story has a happy ending? Should it have ended this way? If you had written this story, how would you have made it end?

Questions for *Jesse's Dream Skirt*

1. Did you like the story? What part did you like best?

2. Have you ever had a dream about something that you wished could happen? Has it ever happened?

3. Do you think it was a good idea for Jesse's mom to make him a skirt like in his dream? Why or why not? Do you think it was a good idea for him to wear the skirt to school? Why or why not?

4. Here's the part where the teacher tells Jesse that it's okay for him to wear his skirt to school. Do you think that the teacher should have let Jesse wear the skirt or should he have made him change into other clothes? What would you do if you were the teacher?

5. Is it okay for girls to wear pants? Why do you think that girls are allowed to wear pants but boys aren't supposed to wear skirts? Do you think that's right? Would you like it better if

girls and boys could wear anything they wanted or do you like it the way it is now?

6. Why do you think the other children teased Jesse and called him a sissy? What do you think the word 'sissy' means? Do you think that it was right of the other children to laugh at Jesse and make fun of him? If a boy in your class wore a skirt to school, would you laugh at him and call him a sissy? What would you do?

7. Can you think of any time that a boy or man might wear a dress? Is it okay if boys try on their mother's or their sister's dresses? *Boys:* Do you ever wear a dress or a skirt at home? Does your mom/sister? Does your dad/brother? Would you ever wear a skirt if your mom or dad let you? Would it matter to you if your friends saw you wearing a dress or skirt?

8. Do you think that this story has a happy ending? Do you think that it should have ended this way? If you had written this story, how would you have made it end?

Questions for *The Girl Who Would Rather Climb Trees*

1. Did you like the story? What part did you like best?

2. When you're playing, what kinds of things do you like to do? Why do you like doing that? Are there any games or toys that you think are just for girls? Just for boys?

3. On this page it says, "Melissa is pretty much an all-around girl." What do you think that means? What kinds of things do you think an "all-around girl" would do? What kinds of things would an "all-around boy" do?

4. Do you think that, at the beginning of this story, Melissa liked playing with her doll? What about at the end of the story? Would you like to get a doll as a present? (*If yes*) What kind would you like to have? What would you do with a doll? (*If no*) If someone gave you a doll as a present, would you play with it? Why or why not?

5. Do you think that a doll would be a good present to give to a girl? To a boy? Is there any present that would be better? Would a doll be a good present to give to a baby girl? A baby

boy? Do you think that it's a good idea for girls to play with dolls? Why or why not? Do you think that it's a good idea for boys to play with dolls? Why or why not?

6. If you could have any game or toy as a present, what would you ask for?

7. Are most of your friends boys or girls or both boys and girls? What kinds of things do you do with your friends? Have any friends ever said to you, "Only girls/boys (*opposite sex of child*) play that" or "That's a girl/boy (*opposite sex of child*) toy?" (*If yes*) What did you do/say to them?

8. Are there any things in this story that you think only girls should do? That only boys should do? Do you think that boys and girls should do the same things? Do you know any boys who like to do girl things? Any girls who like to do boy things? Are they good at doing them?

9. Do you think that it was a good way to end this story? If you had written this story, how would you have made it end?

Appendix B / A Note on Recent Research About Children and Gender

Since gender is a central defining feature of our society, it is not surprising that young children attempt to make it meaningful by distinguishing between girls and boys. The need to identify themselves as being one sex or the other, with no other allowable choices, results from the fact that from the moment of birth, society labels children according to their biological sex, and then continues to differentially reinforce sex-typed behaviours in accordance with these labels—through verbal interactions, physical handling, disciplinary measures, and clothing and toy selection (Davies, 1987; O'Brien & Huston, 1985; O'Brien, Huston & Risley, 1983; Ricks, 1985; Rubin, Provenzano & Luria, 1976; Smith & Daglish, 1977).

Studies show that socialization into appropriate gender roles begins at birth, as girls, wrapped in pink blankets, are treated gently, talked to softly, and described as being dainty, gentle, quiet, and cuddly, while boys are dressed in blue, referred to in terms of being big, strong, and athletic, and handled in a more aggressive, playful manner (Frisch, 1977; Ricks, 1985; Rubin, Provenzano & Luria, 1976). Rothman (1987) suggests that this process may even begin prior to birth. In her study, mothers who learned the sex of their baby through amniocentesis described the male fetus as moving vigorously within the womb and the female fetus as quieter and less energetic, while mothers who did not know the sex of the fetus discussed their pregnancy without describing the baby (p. 129).

Thus, the process that young children undergo in learning how to act within socially-defined gender roles begins when children are labelled by others as either girls or boys (Thompson, 1975). Because our society hides the biological distinctions which would allow children to focus on sexual differences, they come to rely on other characteristics, including differing physical traits, clothing, and behavioural play patterns in order to make sense of what being a boy or being a girl entails (Intons-Peterson, 1988; Pitcher & Schultz, 1983; Kessler & McKenna, 1978). The task of determining how maleness and femaleness are elaborated in the everyday world thus becomes an important one for children; it is the means by which they establish their own genderedness and are perceived by others as being 'normal' functioning members of society (Davies, 1987, p. 41).

Research shows that the way in which children learn to distinguish between the two sexes is the result of a variety of socializing agents that are influential within the home and community environments in which children are raised (Laws, 1979; Lever, 1978). The number of adult males and females in their lives and the roles these adults model (Etaugh, 1983; Langlois & Downs, 1980), the biological sex of older or younger siblings (Stoneman, Brody & MacKinnon, 1986; Sutton-Smith & Rosenberg, 1979), the degree to which access to media, especially television, is allowed (Carlsson-Paige & Levin, 1990; Hyde, 1984a; Sternglanz & Serbin, 1974) are just a few of the influences affecting children's views of themselves as gendered beings.

Other researchers emphasize the importance of the peer group in reinforcing children's understanding of genderedness (Blomberg, 1981; Carter & McCloskey, 1983; Lever, 1976, 1978). Lever's studies (1976, 1978) explore the influence of the peer group as a socializing agent and play as a socializing activity. Her findings show that as children become involved with a peer group, their impressions are coloured by the behaviours of those around them; they begin to test out their beliefs against those of their friends, to imitate the behaviours of others, and in collusion with their peers, to develop a set of tacit rules about how boys or girls should act. She suggests that the differences in play behaviours in childhood are linked to the development of social skills and capacities which, in turn, are important for the performance of male and female adult roles in society (1976, p. 484).

Because of their need to become increasingly familiar with the set of social conventions already in place, it is not surprising that by the time of school entry at three or four years of age, young children have already developed specific notions about differences between boys and girls. Upon starting school, although the home environment continues to be important, influences within the school environment also become powerful socializing agents in children's lives. The strongest influences within the educational setting appear to be teachers and principals, instructional materials (including both books and toys) and exposure to a larger, more varied peer group (Fischer & Cheyne, 1977; Weitzman, 1979).

The biological sex of the teacher and the gendered behaviours displayed within the classroom also affect children's understanding of gender roles. The teacher behaviours which are viewed as being most influential include the following: teachers' reinforcement of distinct male and female roles; whether or not teachers treat girls' and boys' play behaviours differently; the amount of time teachers interact with each sex; the degree to which teachers encourage cross-sex interaction; and teachers' use of gender-specific language within the classroom (Botkin & Twardosz, 1988; Etaugh, 1983; Fagot, 1981; Greenberg, 1985; Hyde, 1984b; Sadker & Sadker, 1982; Serbin, 1978; Serbin, Connor & Citron, 1981). Studies in this area are extensive, dealing with a wide variety of teacher behaviours and student responses. For example, one study found that although girls responded similarly to the presence of male and female preschool teachers in sex-typed activities, boys responded most strongly to male teachers involved in masculine-typed activities (Serbin, Connor & Citron, 1981). Another found that since boys maintain visibility within the classroom environment, girls received less teacher attention than boys unless they stayed physically close to the teacher (Sadker & Sadker, 1982). Even the biological sex of the school principal contributes to children's understanding of gender; in one study, preschool boys in schools with female principals recognized that females could be 'the boss' while boys with male principals did not (Paradise & Wall, 1986).

Instructional materials have also been shown to reinforce or create conflict in children's understanding of gender roles. Choice of classroom toys, along with the means by which children are encouraged to use them, has an impact on both the roles children practise and the academic and life skills they develop (Liss, 1983; Pitcher & Schultz, 1983; Serbin, 1978). For example, studies show that girls often select dolls, thereby reinforcing nurturant, caring roles, parenting skills and verbal expression; or prefer painting, colouring, drawing and doing puzzles, reinforcing fine motor skills and participation in the arts. In contrast, blocks, building toys, and vehicle play are dominated by boys, thereby developing large muscle skills, eye-hand coordination and spatial organization and encouraging explorative, manipulative play (Blomberg, 1981; Eisenberg, 1983; Johnson & Roopnarine, 1983; Serbin, 1978). Based on the abilities and experiences acquired through choice of toy play, when children enter more formal modes of study, boys lean towards maths, sciences, computers, technological studies and aggressive team sports while girls excel in dance, drama, debate, creative writing, reading and the domestic arts (Liss, 1983). Researchers have also noted that different play patterns result depending on whether a toy is verbally presented as being most appropriate for girls, boys or children of both sexes. Toys that were demonstrated by both boys and girls were more often used by all children, even if considered 'male appropriate' or 'female appropriate' by adult standards (Greenberg, 1985, p. 465).

Children's literature, available both at home and within the classroom, also influences the development of gender roles. Educational research continues to stress the importance of children hearing quality literature from infancy (Butler, 1980; Butler & Clay, 1979; Meek, 1982; Taylor & Strickland, 1986). As a result, young children read storybooks over and over again at a time when they are in the process of forming their own gender identities, and may even be exposed to books before being influenced by the external socializing agents of peers, school and teachers. In describing the value of picture books as a source of sex-role learning for young children, Weitzman (1979, p. 7) says: "Through books, children learn about the world outside their immediate environment; they learn what other boys and girls do, say, and feel, and they learn what is expected of children their age."

Unfortunately, children's literature and the reading schemes used within school systems, are often a source of gender bias. Davies (1989c) claims that most texts through which children are taught to read are based on a 'realistic' view in which "the man is presented as active agent in the outside world and the woman as passive, supportive other" (p. 44). Stories are repeatedly dominated by male characters in aggressive, powerful roles, while those female characters who are present are seen as nurturing and submissive to their male counterparts (Batcher, Winter & Wright, 1987; Lobban, 1987; Nilsen, 1977; Petersen & Lach, 1990). A report by the Federation of Women Teachers' Associations of Ontario (1987) examining the sexism of a reading series for young children supports these claims; none of the series was recommended because "a world created and controlled by men, for men, was still the foundation of most stories" (Batcher *et al.*, 1987, p. viii). It thus becomes apparent that the literature chosen for both instructional and recreational purposes within the classroom is an important socializing agent of young children.

References and Further Reading

Aitken, J. (1988). Myth, legend, and fairy tale: "Serious statements about our existence." In *Growing with books (book 1)* (pp. 22-44). Toronto: Ontario Ministry of Education.

Anti-sexist Working Party. (1985). 'Look Jane look': Anti-sexist initiatives in primary schools. In G. Weiner (Ed.), *Just a bunch of girls* (pp. 134-145). Philadelphia: Open University Press.

Applebee, A. (1978). *The child's concept of story: Ages two to seventeen.* Chicago: University of Chicago Press.

Askew, S. & Ross, C. (1988). *Boys don't cry.* Philadelphia: Open University Press.

Ayim, M. (1985). Genderized education: Tradition reconsidered. *Educational Theory, 35,* 345-350.

Barrow, R. (1984). *Giving teaching back to teachers.* London, ON: The Althouse Press.

Batcher, E., Brackstone, D., Winter, A. & Wright, V. (1987). *And then there were none.* Toronto: Federation of Women Teachers' Association of Ontario.

Bem, S. (1983). Gender schema theory and its implications for child development: Raising gender-aschematic children in a gender-schematic society. *Signs, 8,* 598-616.

Berk, L. & Lewis, N. (1977). Sex role and social behaviour in four school environments. *Elementary School Journal, 77*(3), 204-217.

Best, R. (1983). *We've all got scars: What boys and girls learn in elementary school.* Bloomington: Indiana University Press.

Bettelheim, B. (1975). Some further thoughts on the doll corner. *School Review, 83,* 363-368.

Bleich, D. (1986). Gender interests in reading and language. In E. Flynn & P. Schweickart (Eds.), *Gender and reading: Essays on readers, texts and contexts* (pp. 234-266). Baltimore: John Hopkins University Press.

Blomberg, J. (1981). *Sex-typed channelling behaviour in the pre-school peer group: A study of toy choice in same-sex and cross-sex play.* Unpublished doctoral dissertation, University of California, Berkeley.

Botkin, D. & Twardosz, S. (1988). Early childhood teachers' affectionate behavior: Differential expression to female children, male children, and groups of children. *Early Childhood Research Quarterly, 3,* 167-177.

Bredemeier, B., Shields, D., Weiss, M. & Cooper, B. (1986). The relationship of sport involvement with children's moral reasoning and aggression tendencies. *Journal of Sport Psychology, 8,* 304-318.

Browne, N. & France, P. (1985). 'Only sissies wear dresses': A look at sexist talk in the nursery. In G. Weiner (Ed.), *Just a bunch of girls* (pp. 146-159). Philadelphia: Open University Press.

Browne, N. & France, P. (1986). Unclouded minds saw unclouded visions: Visual images in the nursery. In N. Browne & P. France (Eds.), *Untying the apron strings: Anti-sexist provision for the under fives* (pp. 121-141). Philadelphia: Open University Press.

Bruce, W. (1985). The implications of sex role stereotyping in the first years of school. *Australian Journal of Early Childhood, 10,* 48-52.

Burn, E. (1989). Inside the Lego house. In C. Skelton (Ed.), *Whatever happens to little women?: Gender and primary schooling* (pp. 139-148). Philadelphia: Open University Press.

Butler, D. (1980). *Babies need books.* Middlesex: Penguin.

Butler, D. & Clay, M. (1979). *Reading begins at home.* Auckland: Heinemann.

Campbell, B. (1987). *A review of the promotional hopes and aspirations of women in Queensland primary schools.* Unpublished master's thesis, University of New England, Australia.

Carlsson-Paige, N. & Levin, D. (1990). *Who's calling the shots?: How to respond effectively to children's fascination with war play and war toys.* Philadelphia: New Society Publishers.

Carter, D.B. & McCloskey, L.A. (1983). Peers and the maintenance of sex-typed behavior: The development of children's conceptions of cross-gender behavior in their peers. *Social Cognition, 2,* 294-314.

Cherry, L.J. (1979). A sociocognitive approach to language development and its implications for education. In O. Garnica & M. King (Eds.), *Language, children and society: The effect of social factors on children learning to communicate* (pp. 115-134). Toronto: Pergamon Press.

Claricoates, K. (1987). Child culture at school: A clash between gendered worlds? In A. Pollard (Ed.), *Children and their primary schools: A new perspective* (pp. 188-206). Philadelphia: Falmer Press.

Clark, M. (1989). Anastasia is a normal developer because she is unique. *Oxford Review of Education, 15*, 243-255.

Davies, B. (1982). *Life in the classroom and playground: The accounts of primary school children.* London: Routledge & Kegan Paul.

Davies, B. (1983). The role pupils play in the social construction of classroom order. *British Journal of Sociology of Education, 4*, 55-69.

Davies, B. (1987). The accomplishment of genderedness in pre-school children. In A. Pollard (Ed.), *Children and their primary schools: A new perspective* (pp. 42-57). Philadelphia: Falmer Press.

Davies, B. (1988). *Gender, equity and early childhood.* Canberra: Australia Curriculum Development Centre.

Davies, B. (1989a). The discursive production of the male/female dualism in school settings. *Oxford Review of Education. 15*, 229-241.

Davies, B. (1989b). Education for sexism: A theoretical analysis of the sex/gender bias in education. *Educational Philosophy and Theory, 21*, 1-19.

Davies, B. (1989c). *Frogs and snails and feminist tales: Preschool children and gender.* Sydney: Allen & Unwin.

Davies, L. (1984). *Pupil power: Deviance and gender in school.* Philadelphia: Falmer Press.

Davis, E. (1987). *The liberty cap: A catalogue of non-sexist materials for children.* Chicago: Academy Press.

De Paola, T. (1979). *Oliver Button is a sissy.* New York: Harcourt, Brace & Jovanovich.

Derman-Sparks, L. (1988). *Anti-bias curriculum: Tools for empowering young children.* Washington: National Association for the Education of Young Children.

Eisenberg, N. (1983). Sex-typed toy choices: What do they signify? In M.B. Liss (Ed.), *Social and cognitive skills: Sex roles and children's play* (pp. 45-70). New York: Academic Press.

Etaugh, C. (1983). The influence of environmental factors on sex differences in children's play. In M.B. Liss (Ed.), *Social and cognitive skills: Sex roles and children's play.* New York: Academic Press.

Etaugh, C. & Riley, S. (1979). Knowledge of sex stereotypes in preschool children. *Psychological Reports, 44*, 1279-1282.

Evans, T. (1982). Being and becoming: Teachers' perceptions of sex-roles and actions toward their male and female pupils. *British Journal of Sociology of Education, 3*, 127-143.

Fagot, B. (1981). Male and female teachers: Do they treat boys and girls differently? *Sex Roles, 7*, 263-271.

Fagot, B. & Leinbach, M.D. (1983). Play styles in early childhood: Social consequences for boys and girls. In M.B. Liss (Ed.), *Social and cognitive skills: Sex roles and children's play* (pp. 93-116). New York: Academic Press.

Favat, A. (1977). *Child and tale: The origins of interest.* Urbana, IL: National Council of Teachers of English.

Fischer, L. & Cheyne, J. (1977). *Sex roles: Biological and cultural interaction as founded in social science research and Ontario educational media.* Toronto: Ministry of Education.

Flynn, E. (1986). Gender and reading. In E. Flynn & P. Schweickart (Eds.), *Gender and reading: Essays on readers, texts and contexts* (pp. 267-288). Baltimore: John Hopkins University Press.

Frazier, N. & Sadker, M. (1973). *Sexism in school and society.* New York: Harper & Row.

Freebody, P. & Baker, C. (1985). Children's first schoolbooks: Introductions to the culture of literacy. *Harvard Educational Review, 55*(4), 381-398.

French, J. (1984). Gender imbalances in the primary classroom: An interactional account. *Educational Research, 6,* 127-136.

Frieze, I., Parson, J., Johnson, P., Ruble, D. & Zellman, G. (1978). *Women and sex roles: A social psychological perspective.* New York: W.W. Norton.

Frisch, H. (1977). Sex stereotypes in adult-infant play. *Child Development, 48,* 1671-1675.

Galda, L. & Pellegrini, A.D. (Eds.). (1985). *Play, language and stories: The development of children's literate behavior.* Norwood, NJ: Ablex.

Garnica, O. (1979). The boys have the muscles and the girls have the sexy legs: Adult-child speech and the use of generic person labels. In O. Garnica & M. King (Eds.), *Language, children and society: The effect of social factors on children learning to communicate* (pp. 135-148). Toronto: Pergamon Press.

Gaskell, J., McLaren, A. & Novogrodsky, M. (1989). *Claiming an education: Feminism and Canadian schools.* Toronto: Our Schools/ Our Selves Education Foundation.

Gilbert, P. (1989). Personally (and passively) yours: Girls literacy and education. *Oxford Review of Education, 15,* 257-265.

Gleason, J.B. (1979). Sex differences in the language of children and parents. In O. Garnica & M. King (Eds.), *Language, children and society: The effect of social factors on children learning to communi-*

cate (pp. 149-157). Toronto: Pergamon Press.

Gould, L. (1972). X: A fabulous child's story. *Ms, 1*(6), 74-76, 105, 106.

Greenberg, S. (1985), Educational equity in early education environments. In S. Klein (Ed.), *Handbook for achieving sex equity through education.* Baltimore: John Hopkins University Press.

Grief, E.B. (1976). Sex role playing in pre-school children. In J.S. Bruner, A. Jolly & K. Sylva (Eds.), *Play, its role in development and evolution* (pp. 385-391). New York: Basic Books.

Griffith, A.I. & Smith, D.E. (1986). Constructing cultural knowledge: Mothering as discourse. In J. Gaskell & A. McLaren (Eds.), *Women and education: A Canadian perspective* (pp. 87-103). Calgary: Detselig Enterprises.

Harste, J.C., Woodward, V.A. & Burke, C.L. (1984). *Language stories and literacy lessons.* Portsmouth, NH: Heinemann.

Holdaway, D. (1979). *The foundations of literacy.* Toronto: Ashton-Scholastic.

Houston, B. (1985). Gender freedom and the subtleties of sexist education. *Educational Theory, 35*(4), 359-369.

Houston, B. (1989). Theorizing gender: How much of it do we need? *Educational Philosophy and Theory, 21*(1), 20, 24-30.

Hyde, J. (1984a). Children's understanding of sexist language. *Developmental Psychology, 20*, 697-704.

Hyde, J. (1984b). How large are gender differences in aggression?: A developmental meta-analysis. *Developmental Psychology, 20*, 722-736.

Intons-Peterson, M.J. (1988). *Children's concepts of gender.* Norwood, NJ: Ablex.

Iso-ahola, S. (1979). Sex-role stereotypes and causal attributions for success and failure in motor performance. *Research Quarterly, 50*, 630-640.

Jackson, S. (1982). *Childhood and sexuality.* Oxford: Blackwell.

Jaggar, A. & Smith-Burke, M.T. (Eds.). (1985). *Observing the language learner.* Urbana, IL: National Council of Teachers of English.

Johnson, J.E. & Roopnarine, J.L. (1983). The preschool classroom and sex differences in children's play. In M.B. Liss (Ed.), *Social and cognitive skills: Sex roles and children's play.* New York: Academic Press.

Johnson, M. (1967). Definitions and models in curriculum theory. *Educational Theory, 17*, 127-140.

Katz, L. (1978). Teacher education and non-sexist early childhood education. In B. Sprung (Ed.), *Perspectives in non-sexist early childhood education* (pp. 57-61). New York: Teachers College Press.

Kennard, J. (1986). Ourself beyond ourself: A theory for lesbian readers. In E. Flynn and P. Schweickhart (Eds.), *Gender and reading: Essays on readers, texts and contexts*. Baltimore: John Hopkins University Press.

Kessler, S. & McKenna, W. (1978). *Gender: An ethnomethodological approach*. New York: John Wiley & Sons.

Kidd, B. (1987). Sports and masculinity. In M. Kaufman (Ed.), *Beyond patriarchy: Essays by men*, London: Oxford University Press.

Kincheloe, J.L. (1991). *The teacher as researcher*. Philadelphia: Falmer Press.

Kohlberg, L. (1966). A cognitive-developmental analysis of children's role concepts and attitudes. In E.E. Maccoby (Ed.), *The development of sex differences* (pp. 82-173). Stanford, CA: Stanford University Press.

Langlois, J. & Downs, C. (1980). Mothers, fathers and peers as socialization agents of sex-typed play behaviours in children. *Child Development, 51*, 1237-1247.

Laws, J. (1979). *The second x: Sex role and socialization role*. New York: Elsevier North Holland.

Lever, J. (1976). Sex differences in the games children play. *Social Problems, 23*, 479-487.

Lever, J. (1978). Sex differences in the complexity of children's play and games. *American Sociological Review, 43*, 471-483.

Lima, C.W. (1986). *A to zoo: Subject access to children's picture books*. New York: R.R. Bowker.

Lincoln, Y. & Guba, E. (1985). *Naturalistic inquiry*. Beverly Hills, CA: Sage Publications.

Lincoln, Y. & Guba, E. (1982). *Effective evaluation: Improving the usefulness of evaluation results through responsive and naturalistic approaches*. San Francisco: Jossey-Bass.

Liss, M.B. (1983). Learning gender-related skills through play. In M.B. Liss (Ed.), *Social and cognitive skills: Sex roles and children's play* (pp. 147-167). New York: Academic Press.

Lobban, G. (1987). Sex roles in reading schemes. In G. Weiner & M. Arnot (Eds.), *Gender under scrutiny: New inquiries into education* (pp. 150-154). London: Hutchinson, in association with the Open University.

Mack, B. (1979). *Jesse's dream skirt*. Chapel Hill, NC: Lollipop Power.

MacLean, A. (1972). *The idea of God in protestant religious education*. New York: Teachers College Press.

Mahony, P. (1983). How Alice's chin really came to be pressed against her foot: Sexist processes of interaction in mixed-sex classrooms. *Women's Studies International Forum, 6*, 107-115.

McRobbie, A. (1986). Dance and social fantasy. In G. Nelson (Ed.), *Theory in the classroom* (pp. 130-161). Urbana: University of Illinois Press.

Meek, M. (1982). *Learning to read*. London: Bodley Head.

Minuchin, P. (1976). Sex-role concepts and sex typing in childhood as a function of school and home environments. In A. Kaplan & J. Bean (Eds.), *Beyond sex stereotyping: Readings towards a psychology of androgyny*. Toronto: Little, Brown and Company.

Monagan, D. (1983, March). The failure of co-ed sports. *Psychology Today*, pp. 58-63.

Money, J. & Ehrhardt, A. (1972). *Man and woman, boy and girl*. Baltimore: John Hopkins University Press.

Money, J. & Tucker, P. (1975). *Sexual signatures: On being a man or a woman*. Boston: Little, Brown & Company.

Morgan, K. & Ayim, M. (1984). Comment on Bem's 'Raising gender-aschematic children in a gender-schematic society'. *Signs, 10*, 189-199.

Munsch, R. (1980). *The paper bag princess*. Toronto: Annick Press.

Nemerowicz, G. (1979). *Children's perceptions of gender and work roles*. New York: Praeger.

Nichols, J. (1975). Causal attributions and other achievement-related cognitions: Effects of task outcome, attainment value and sex. *Journal of Personality and Social Psychology, 31*, 379-389.

Nilsen, A. (1977). Sexism in children's books and elementary classroom materials. In A. Nilsen, H. Bosmajian, H. Gershneny & J. Stanley (Eds.), *Sexism and language* (pp.161-179). Urbana, IL: National Council of Teachers of English.

O'Brien, M. & Huston, A.C. (1985). Development of sex-typed play behavior in toddlers. *Developmental Psychology, 21*, 866-871.

O'Brien, M., Huston, A. & Risley, T. (1983). Sex-typed play of toddlers in a day care centre. *Journal of Applied Developmental Psychology, 4*, 1-9.

Paley, V. (1973). Is the doll corner a sexist institution? *School Review, 81*, 569-576.

Paley, V. (1984). *Boys and girls: Superheroes in the doll corner*. Chicago: University of Chicago Press.

Paley, V. (1988). *Bad guys don't have birthdays: Fantasy play at four*. Chicago: University of Chicago Press.

Paradise, L. & Wall, S. (1986). Children's perceptions of male and female principals and teachers. *Sex Roles, 14*, 1-7.

Parlett, M. & Hamilton, D. (1977). Evaluation as illumination: A new approach to the study of innovatory programmes. In D. Hamilton, B. Macdonald & C. King (Eds.), *Beyond the numbers: A reader in educational evaluation* (pp. 6-22). Berkeley, CA: McCutchan.

Patton, M. (1980). *Qualitative evaluation methods.* Beverly Hills, CA: Sage Publications.

Peirce, K. & Edwards, E.D. (1988). Children's construction of fantasy stories: Gender differences in conflict resolution strategies. *Sex Roles, 18*, 393-404.

Peterson, S.B. & Lach, M.A. (1990). Gender stereotypes in children's books: Their prevalence and influence on cognitive and affective development. *Gender and Education, 2*, 185-197.

Pitcher, E.G. & Schultz, L.H. (1983). *Boys and girls at play: The development of sex roles.* South Hadley, MA: Bergin & Garvey.

Pratt, D. (1980). *Curriculum: Design and development.* New York: Harcourt, Brace & Jovanovich.

Reinharz, S. (1979). *On becoming a social scientist.* San Francisco: Jossey-Bass.

Reis, H.T. & Wright, S. (1982). Knowledge of sex-role stereotypes in children aged 3 to 5. *Sex Roles, 8*, 1049-1056.

Ricks, S. (1985). Father-infant interactions: A review of empirical research. *Family Relations, 34*, 505-511.

Robinson, E. (1983). *The original vision: A study of the religious experience of childhood.* New York: Seabury Press.

Rosen, H. (1986). The importance of story. *Language Arts, 63*, 226-237.

Rothman, B. (1987). *The tentative pregnancy: Prenatal diagnosis and the future of motherhood.* New York: Penguin.

Rubin, J., Provenzano, F. & Luria, Z. (1976). The eye of the beholder: Parents' views on sex of newborns. *American Journal of Orthopsychiatry, 44*, 512-519.

Sadker, M. & Sadker, D. (1982). *Sex equity handbook for schools.* New York: Longman.

Schacher, W. (Ed.). (1976). *A guide to non-sexist children's books.* Chicago: Academy Press.

Schlein, M. (1975). *The girl who would rather climb trees.* New York: Harcourt, Brace & Jovanovich.

Segel, E. (1986). "As the twig is bent...": Gender and childhood reading. In E. Flynn & P. Schweickart (Eds.), *Gender and reading: Essays on readers, texts and contexts* (pp. 165-186). Baltimore: John Hopkins University.

Serbin, L. (1978). Teachers, peers, and play preferences: An environmental approach to sex typing in the preschool. In B. Sprung (Ed.), *Perspectives in non-sexist early childhood education* (pp. 79-93). New York: Teachers College Press.

Serbin, L., Connor, J. & Citron, C. (1981). Sex differentiated free play behaviour: Effects of teacher modelling, location and gender. *Developmental Psychology, 17,* 640-646.

Serbin, L. & Sprafkin, C. (1986). The salience of gender and the process of sex typing in three to seven year-old children. *Child Development, 57,* 1188-1199.

Short, G. & Carrington, B. (1989). Discourse on gender: The perceptions of children aged between six and eleven. In C. Skelton (Ed.), *Whatever happens to little women?: Gender and primary schooling* (pp. 22-37). Philadelphia: Open University Press.

Smith P. & Daglish, L. (1977). *Children's concepts of gender.* Norwood, NJ: Ablex.

Spender, D. (1989). *Invisible women: The schooling scandal.* London: Women's Press.

Spender, D. & Sarah, E. (Eds.). (1980). *Learning to lose: Sexism and education.* London: Women's Press.

Sprafkin, C., Serbin, L., Denier, C. & Connor, J. (1983). Sex-differentiated play: Cognitive consequences and early interventions. In M.B. Liss (Ed.), *Social and cognitive skills: Sex roles and children's play.* New York: Academic Press.

Stacey, J., Bereaud, S. & Daniels, J. (1974). *And Jill came tumbling after: Sexism in American education.* New York: Dell.

Sternglanz, S. & Serbin, L. (1974). Sex role stereotyping in children's television programs. *Developmental Psychology, 10,* 710-715.

Stonemen, Z., Brody, G. & MacKinnon, C. (1986). Same-sex and cross-sex siblings: Activity choices, roles, behaviours and gender stereotypes. *Sex Roles, 15,* 495-511.

Strike, K. (1977). Liberality and censorship: A philosophy of textbook controversies. *Philosophy of Education.* Proceedings of the 33rd Annual Meeting of the Philosophy of Education Society (pp. 277-286). Worchester, MA: Heffernan Press.

Sutton-Smith, B. & Rosenberg, B. (1979). *The sibling.* New York: Riley Press.

Tavris, C. & Baumgartner, A. (1983). How would your life be different if you'd been born a boy? *Redbook, 160,* 92-95.

Taylor, D. & Strickland, D. (1986). *Family storybook reading.* Toronto: Scholastic.

Taylor, R.D. & Carter, D.B. (1987). The association between children's gender understanding, sex-role knowledge, and sex-role preferences. *Child Study Journal, 17*, 185-196.

Tetenbaum, T.J. & Pearson, J. (1989). The voices in children's literature: The impact of gender on the moral decisions of storybook characters. *Sex Roles, 20*, 381-393.

Thomas, G. (1986). 'Hallo, Miss Scatterbrain. Hallo, Mr. Strong': Assessing attitude and behaviour in the nursery. In N. Browne & P. France (Eds.), *Untying the apron strings: Anti-sexist provision for the under fives* (pp. 104-120). Philadelphia: Open University Press.

Thompson, S. (1975). Gender labels and early sex role development. *Child Development, 46*, 339-347.

Trepanier, M.L. & Romatowski, J.A. (1985). Attributes and roles assigned to characters in children's writing: Sex differences and sex-role perceptions. *Sex Roles, 13*, 263-272.

Tutchell, E. (1990). *Dolls and dungarees: Gender issues in the primary school curriculum.* Philadelphia: Open University Press.

Urberg, K.A. (1982). The development of the concepts of masculinity and femininity in young children. *Sex roles, 8*, 659-668.

Walkerdine, V. (1984). Some day my prince will come. In A. McRobbie & M. Nava (Eds.), *Gender and generation* (pp. 162-184). London: Macmillan.

Walkerdine, V. (1989). Femininity as performance. *Oxford Review of Education, 15*, 267-279.

Walkerdine, V. & Lucey, H. (1989). *Democracy in the kitchen: Regulating mothers and socializing daughters.* London: Virago.

Weitzman, L. (1979). *Sex role socialization: A focus on women.* Palo Alto, CA: Mayfield.

Wells, G. (1985). *Language, learning and education.* Philadelphia: NFER-Nelson.

Wilms, D. & Cooper, I. (1987). *A guide to non-sexist children's books.* Chicago: Academy Press.

Zipes, J. (1982). The potential of liberating fairy tales for children. *New Literary History, 13*, 309-325.

Zipes, J. (1986). *Don't bet on the prince: Contemporary feminist fairy tales in North America and England.* Aldershot, EN: Gower.

Zuckerman, D.M. & Sayre, D.H. (1982). Cultural sex-role expectations and children's sex-role concepts. *Sex Roles, 8*, 853-862.

Index of Authors

AITKEN, J., 105n, 110n, 123
Applebee, A., 123
Askew, S., 109n, 123
Ayim, M., 123, 129

BAKER, C., 110n, 126
Barrow, R., 110n, 123
Batcher, E., 110n, 121, 123
Baumgartner, A., 131
Bem, S., 123
Bereaud, S., 105n, 131
Berk, L., 92, 109n, 110n, 123
Best, R., 105n, 109n, 123
Bettelheim, B., 108n, 123
Bleich, D., 123
Blomberg, J., 118, 120, 124
Botkin, D., 119, 124
Brackstone, D., 110n, 123
Bredemeier, B., 47, 107n, 124
Brody, G., 118, 131
Browne, N., 124
Bruce, W., 105n, 109n, 124
Burke, C.L., 105n, 127
Burn, E., 124
Butler, D., 120, 124

CAMPBELL, B., 110n, 124
Carlsson-Paige, N., 31, 41, 43, 46, 107n, 108n, 109n, 118, 124
Carrington, B., 131
Carter, D.B., 118, 124, 132
Cherry, L.J., 124
Cheyne, J., 119, 126
Citron, C., 119, 131
Claricoates, K., 124

Clark, M., 125
Clay, M., 120, 124
Connor, J., 119, 131
Cooper, B., 107n
Cooper, I., 106n, 124, 132

DAGLISH, L., 117, 131
Daniels, J., 105n, 109n, 131
Davies, B., 8, 12, 13, 14, 53, 63, 72, 74, 84, 90, 92, 105n, 107n, 108n, 109n, 110n, 118, 121, 125
Davies, L., 125
Davis, E., 106n, 125
Denier, C., 131
De Paola, T., 21, 125
Derman-Sparks, L., 125
Downs, C., 118, 128

EDWARDS, E.D., 130
Ehrhardt, A., 129
Eisenberg, N., 120, 125
Etaugh, C., 118, 119, 125
Evans, T., 110n, 125

FAGOT, B., 119, 125, 126
Favat, A., 11, 105n, 126
Fischer, L., 119, 126
Flynn, E., 126
France, P., 124
Frazier, N., 126
Freebody, P., 110n, 126
French, J., 126
Frieze, I., 126
Frisch, H., 117, 126